Sermons to Self

Sermons to Self

Touching God

Christopher Ward

RESOURCE *Publications* • Eugene, Oregon

SERMONS TO SELF
Touching God

Copyright © 2014 Christopher Ward. All rights reserved. Except for brief quotations in critical publications or reviews, no part of this book may be reproduced in any manner without prior written permission from the publisher. Write: Permissions. Wipf and Stock Publishers, 199 W. 8th Ave., Suite 3, Eugene, OR 97401.

Wipf and Stock
An Imprint of Wipf and Stock Publishers
199 W. 8th Ave., Suite 3
Eugene, OR 97401

www.wipfandstock.com

ISBN 13: 978-1-4982-0421-7

Manufactured in the U.S.A.   11/13/2014

All Bible quotations are taken from the Revised English Bible, copyright © Cambridge University Press and Oxford University Press 1989. All rights reserved.

Contents

Preface | ix
Introduction | xiii

First Sunday of Advent – Anticipation and Expectation | 1

Second Sunday of Advent – New World Order | 4

Third Sunday of Advent – Patience | 7

Fourth Sunday of Advent – Believing the Unbelievable | 10

Christmas Day – Trappings, Traditions and Words | 13

First Sunday of Christmas – Testing Times | 16

Second Sunday of Christmas – Grace, Truth and Rejection | 19

The Epiphany – Birth and Death | 22

The Baptism of Christ (First Sunday of Epiphany) – Start of Life's Work | 25

Second Sunday of Epiphany – Conundrums of Calling | 28

Third Sunday of Epiphany – Rhetoric and Reason | 31

The Presentation of Christ in the Temple (Candlemas) – Struggling Thoughts | 34

Fourth Sunday before Lent – Salt and Spirit | 37

Third Sunday before Lent – Tough Talking | 40

Second Sunday before Lent – Creation and Anxiety | 43

CONTENTS

Sunday next before Lent – Clouds of Not Knowing | 46

Ash Wednesday – Ritual Reminders | 49

First Sunday of Lent – Tempting Offers | 52

Second Sunday of Lent – Uncomfortable Words | 55

Third Sunday of Lent – Meat and Drink | 58

Annunciation of our Lord to the Blessed Virgin Mary – Questioning Acceptance | 61

Fourth Sunday of Lent – Seeing and Believing | 64

Fifth Sunday of Lent – Sorrowful Doubts | 67

Palm Sunday – Triumph and Tragedy | 70

Maundy Thursday – Significant Acts | 73

Good Friday – Truth and Betrayal | 76

Easter Day – Loss and Discovery | 79

Second Sunday of Easter – Beyond Doubt | 82

Third Sunday of Easter – Excited Understanding | 85

Fourth Sunday of Easter – Herd Instincts | 88

Fifth Sunday of Easter – Paths to Truth | 91

Sixth Sunday of Easter – Groping in the Dark | 94

Ascension Day – Rising to New Heights | 97

Seventh Sunday of Easter/Sunday after Ascension Day – Humble Knowledge | 100

Day of Pentecost/Whit Sunday – Varieties of Gifts | 103

Trinity Sunday – What About God? | 106

First Sunday after Trinity – Losing and Finding | 109

Second Sunday after Trinity – Prophets of Good | 112

Third Sunday after Trinity – Burdens of Guilt | 115

Fourth Sunday after Trinity – Fruitful Seeds | 118

Contents

Fifth Sunday after Trinity – Mixed Messages | 121
Sixth Sunday after Trinity – Painful Images | 124
Seventh Sunday after Trinity – Enough Food | 127
Eighth Sunday after Trinity – Storms of Faith | 130
Ninth Sunday after Trinity – Crumbs of Learning | 133
Tenth Sunday after Trinity – Skills and Belief | 136
Eleventh Sunday after Trinity – Harsh Words | 139
Twelfth Sunday after Trinity – Love and Orgies | 142
Thirteenth Sunday after Trinity – Forgiving Ourselves | 145
Fourteenth Sunday after Trinity – Personal Worth | 148
Fifteenth Sunday after Trinity – Real Authority | 151
Sixteenth Sunday after Trinity – Proper Fruit | 154
Seventeenth Sunday after Trinity – Reluctant Guests | 157
Eighteenth Sunday after Trinity – Paying Our Dues | 160
Last Sunday after Trinity – Sales Talk | 163
All Saints Day – Personal Failures | 166
Fourth Sunday before Advent – Ends and Beginnings | 169
Third Sunday before Advent – Be Prepared | 172
Second Sunday before Advent – Hidden Talents | 175
Sunday next before Advent – Touching God | 178

Conclusions | 181
Index of Bible Extracts | 185
Index of Themes | 189

Preface

THE UNEXPECTED INSPIRATION FOR this book came from *University Challenge*. There was a question about the context of the shortest verse in the Bible—John 11:35, "Jesus wept." The answer was that Jesus was weeping over the death of Lazarus, who he then brought back to life. I was struck by two things: the direct connection between Jesus' feelings and his subsequent action, and the raw power of those two words. Many others have felt the same and recognised that this was a unique expression of Jesus' humanity and of his godliness. My thoughts went in a different direction

From my earliest days the church was part of my life. My father was a Methodist Minister and church attendance every Sunday was both natural and inevitable. I later went to a Methodist public school (Kingswood, in Bath) and attended daily chapel services as we all did. At university (Exeter College, Oxford) I decided that if church attendance was to mean anything to me I wanted it to be in the college chapel rather than the Methodist church, and I became an Anglican. This enthusiasm was not matched by my church attendance which became ever more sporadic until it evaporated altogether, except for a nominal presence at Christmas and Easter. Latterly I have found my rare visits to church deeply frustrating. The liturgy leaves me cold, the preaching leaves me colder, and I have no sense of the warmth of a church community. I have sat, and listened, and taken part (reading lessons, taking communion), but feeling more and more that this has no meaning for me. Yet I have long wanted it to have a meaning.

There was too much in my upbringing, my education, my personal beliefs, my understanding of the important things in life, for me to reject Christianity altogether. I wanted to say, "I believe, help thou my unbelief," but I wasn't sure who I was talking to or why. I wanted to find a way in to thinking about Christianity more deeply, exploring my beliefs and unbelief, and exchanging a dilettante flirtation with things religious for deeper consideration.

PREFACE

I wanted to reach a point where I could say more confidently, "That is what I believe," even if that was a turning away from Christianity altogether.

Objectively I knew that there were a number of paths I could follow: serious reading, discussion, work with like-minded groups, even gritting my teeth to "go to church," but subjectively I found the commitment to any of these very difficult. Was this laziness, apathy, or commitment-phobia? I wasn't sure. Probably all three, and others besides. I wanted to get on with it, but just didn't. Until *University Challenge*.

"Jesus wept" made sense to me. I was struck by the fact that these two words had survived numerous translations and scholarship. Their sheer brevity was extraordinary, yet they had an impact at many levels. I heard them as if for the first time, despite the bizarre circumstances of an upmarket television quiz show. They made me think.

Perhaps the "way in" was not to struggle with Christian belief, faith, observance and practice but to go back to basics and to concentrate on those moments, in the midst of arid liturgy, hard pews, and patronising preaching, when words from the Bible suddenly came alive.

I looked back over my life and thought about all the Sundays, and other days, when I have listened to a reading from the Old Testament, said or sung a Psalm, listened to the Epistle, and stood for the Gospel. Regular church attendance from the age of 10 to 60 would mean hearing over 10,000 Bible readings. My own experience would be barely 20 percent of that, but I knew that while repetition had built a lasting memory, familiarity had bred, if not contempt, a feeling that these words were largely empty, for me. That was my emotional reaction.

Intellectually, I really enjoyed "thinking about things religious." I was fascinated by the struggle to make sense of biblical imagery, metaphor and allusion, but frustrated by clergy who destroyed that by simplistic retelling or over-academic cross-referencing and semantic unpacking. I wanted the Bible to make sense to me now, some way, somehow. Its importance had to be personal to me, in the here and now, not because of its hallowed history.

I decided that the way forward was to use the example of "Jesus wept" and systematically look for those passages that might strike a chord with me now. Trying to read the Bible from cover to cover would certainly be counter-productive. Boredom would set in and prevent any intellectual and emotional response to the words. So I decided to replicate the experience in church.

PREFACE

I used the Common Worship Lectionary for 2014 and over a number of weeks, early that same year, I read every Old Testament, Psalm, Epistle and Gospel reading appointed for each Sunday and Principal Feasts and Holy Days. Whilst many were familiar, I had no idea what to expect as I looked up each reading. I did my best to gauge the impact of each. I then wrote down the three verses that had struck me most forcibly, without worrying over much why.

Then I read all the passages a second time. In most cases this confirmed my choice of verses, but in some I discovered new emphasis or importance, so I made some changes, either replacing or extending my original choice.

Choosing three verses, or sets of verses, for each Sunday was entirely arbitrary. Surprisingly this turned out to be a good number as it maintained impact while providing a variety of contrasting or complementary ideas.

My plan then was to use these three sets of verses for a personal exploration against each Sunday in the year of why they seemed important to me at the time. These were to be my "sermons to self."

I had no idea whether this would lead me to a deeper understanding of the Christian faith and a strengthening of my Christian belief or to an even greater indifference or even rejection of both.

Christopher Ward
Easter 2014

Introduction

"Ask, and you will receive; seek, and you will find; knock and the door will be opened to you. For everyone who asks receives, those who seek find, and to those who knock the door will be opened."

MATTHEW 7:7

I HAVE ALWAYS BELIEVED that God does indeed work in a mysterious way—how could he not—and the mystery lies in the unexpected. We may not receive quite what we ask for, or in the way we expected to receive it. Our search may lead us to find things we had never thought of. Our knocking may be on the wrong door, or the right door may open long after our knocking has ceased. It will be interesting to see how true this is.

This book is my own "exploration" and "search." The Oxford Concise Dictionary (OCD) definition of "explore" is to "travel (though an unfamiliar area) in order to learn about it." That is close to where I am. There may be something interesting out there, though I am not sure where, or when I will find it. My natural curiosity and restlessness makes me want to go looking for it. I have set the parameters—the Bible readings for every Sunday in 2014—but these are fairly arbitrary. There is a reasonable argument that looking in the Bible is a good place to start, but there is no guarantee that I will find what I am looking for there. Many would argue that the Bible is the only place to look. I do not share that belief. My personal hope, at the start, is that it will offer me food for thought, pointers to paths that I might follow, and quite possibly new insights. I have no idea whether this will turn out to be the case.

"Search," again according to the OCD, means to "try to find something by looking or otherwise seeking carefully and thoroughly." That is a much more focussed activity. Searching without an object is pointless. There has to be a "something." My problem is that I am not sure what that something is. A confirmation of the validity and value of the Christian faith? Robust arguments to bolster my own wavering faith? An understanding of God? Radical rethinking that will negate any religious faith and put an end to the wavering? It could be any of those.

The fundamental point is that this exploration and search is something that I believe I have to do. Not to address something that in my heart I believe is important would be a personal failure and betrayal.

It is very easy to be led astray. Attractive pathways beckon, unexpected vistas open up, evocative memories obscure the view, opportunities to linger longer in certain places arise, and outward appearances belie inner truths. Some ground rules are needed:

Audience

The "sermons" are to me in the first instance. They may be of interest to a wider audience, but they are not written for or to others. These are my views from the pew, not to the pews.

Familiarity

Passages from the Bible that I have known since childhood are deeply ingrained and have their own peculiar magic. I must not be seduced by familiar words that engage my emotions but not my thought. My heart must not rule my mind.

Memories

This book covers the whole Christian year. The major festivals have a life time of memories attached to them. These memories are as seductive as the familiar Bible passages that are often closely associated with them. My "view from the pew" must focus on the words and not allow the physical circumstances, whether sacred or secular, to become a substitute for meaning.

INTRODUCTION

Interpretation

All connections, inferences, and interpretations are mine. I have no background in theology or Biblical studies. What I have learned has been "in the pew" or from my own reading. This may well be superficial, inaccurate, or simply wrong, but I am where I am. I must have the courage of my convictions.

Struggle

Christianity has survived because it is capable of interpretation and re-interpretation. Many would argue that in this lies its strength and its depth. Struggling with it is par for the course. I must be prepared to struggle, to work at it, and even then accept that I may not find answers.

First Sunday of Advent
Anticipation and Expectation

Isaiah 2:1–5	Romans 13:11–14
Psalm 122	Matthew 24:36–44

Always remember that this is the hour of crisis: it is high time for you to wake out of sleep, for deliverance is nearer to us now than it was when we first believed. It is far on in the night; day is near. Let us therefore throw off the deeds of darkness, and put on the armour of light.

ROMANS 13:11–12

Keep awake, then, for you do not know on what day your Lord will come. Remember, if the householder had known at what time of night the burglar was coming, he would have stayed awake and not let his house be broken into.

MATTHEW 24:42–43

Hold yourselves ready, therefore, because the Son of Man will come at the time you least expect him.

MATTHEW 24:44

In my pew-sitting days, I was never conscious that the first Sunday in Advent was the start of the Christian year. Guided by the Lectionary I realise now that there is an absolute logic that it should be so. Christ's birth must be a starting point and Advent of course looks forward to that. There is however both a looking back, and a looking even further forward. For me, the latter is easier to engage with than the former. Old Testament writings which "foretell" the coming of Christ, which in the past I have taken at face value, with an almost wilful "suspension of disbelief", now seem less convincing. The eclectic influences and writings that form what we now call The Bible are used to justify a continuity of thought and imagination that while very real two thousand years ago, is now merely historically interesting.

The logic lies in the here and now, not in the then and there. This however is the start of a story whose end we know, whose intermediate chapters are familiar, and whose emotional context has been part of our lives since we understood that Father Christmas was something really to look forward to.

The fact that we know the end of the story gives added poignancy to the beginning. Always at the back of our Christian adult minds is the thought that this birth, unusual if not miraculous in conception and delivery, is full of contrasts: poverty of location against heartfelt and expensive gifts, all the happiness that accompanies any birth against a systematic massacre of young children, and in the end, in all senses of that phrase, a belief that none of this will make sense until the child grows up and is killed. There is more than a hint of menace in the air, bitterness to reduce the sweetness that if allowed to predominate becomes cloying. It is the "Three trees on a low sky" in T.S. Eliot's *Journey of the Magi*. A hint of death to come in the middle of new birth.

The first Sunday in Advent is then a time of expectation. We know what is going to happen and we are looking forward to it. It is also a time of anticipation. Something else is going to happen, and we must be ready for it. So don't get too comfortable.

The three passages above, from Romans and Matthew, emphasise this. Life has moved on. Christ's birth and death are now part of history, but his promise that he would "come again" is a living belief and hope. We can, with some difficulty, think ourselves back to the time when Paul and Matthew were writing, and in so doing we can empathise with them but does a "second coming" hold much meaning for us now?

ANTICIPATION AND EXPECTATION

The Bible passages encourage us to be ready, to keep awake, to behave appropriately, and to recognise that this is the eleventh hour, a very critical time. But what, in the early part of the twenty-first century, are we "keeping awake" for?

I have no expectation of another miraculous birth. That was then, this is now. I have no expectation that some man, or woman, will capture the headlines as the new leader of right-thinking people. It is illuminating however to wonder how such a person would fare in our divided and overpopulated world. How swiftly would he or she be driven into obscurity by secular cynicism, religious intolerance, or the selfish reluctance that lies in all of us to be told what to do?

If we accept (and I am not sure that I do accept this in an absolute and unquestioning way) that God's plan (though the word 'plan' seems pathetically inappropriate) is for the promises initiated by Christ to become and remain real in the lives of everyone, what would be the most effective way of confirming this?

I believe that for each of us this will be different. Some are not troubled by such questions. They have a literalistic belief and an unquestioning faith that provides comforting security.

Others, myself included, are bedevilled by conflicting thoughts, wavering convictions, insubstantial beliefs, emotional ties, and irrational prejudices. We live in hope that we can find a way through this turbulence, or at least find some way of making sense of the storm.

We need guidance, but we may not recognise or accept it when it comes. We seek conviction but are too apathetic to seek it. We are bound to the good and the bad in our upbringing which we are embarrassed to retain or work hard to contradict in our behaviour. We pursue the rational, yet we know that what we talking about goes beyond our mental capacity to understand it. We need a voice crying in our wilderness.

"Keeping awake" then has something to do with expecting the unexpected, recognising that there may be events, people, situations, personal crises that open our eyes to new possibilities that give us new insights. Being ready for these is really the best that we can do, and the best that we can hope to do. The one fact is that in all our lives there are "three trees" that remind us that we are not here for ever. In that case, is trying to make sense of what we are here for, what we are here for?

Second Sunday of Advent
New World Order

Isaiah 11:1–10   Romans 15:4–13
Psalm 72:1–7, 18–19   Matthew 3:1–12

On him the spirit of the Lord will rest: a spirit of wisdom and understanding; a spirit of counsel and power; a spirit of knowledge and fear of the Lord; and in the fear of the Lord will be his delight. He will not judge by outward appearances or decide a case on hearsay; but with justice he will judge the poor and defend the humble in the land with equity; like a rod his verdict will strike the ruthless, and with his word he will slay the wicked. He will wear the belt of justice and truth will be his girdle.

Isaiah 11:2–5

Then the wolf will live with the lamb, and the leopard lie down with the kid; and the calf and the young lion will feed together, with a little child to tend them. The cow and bear will be friends, and their young will lie down together; and the lion will eat straw like cattle. The infant will play over the cobra's hole, and the young child dance over the viper's nest.

Isaiah 11:6–8

NEW WORLD ORDER

> *The scriptures written long ago were all written for our instruction, in order that through the encouragement they give us we maintain our hope with perseverance.*
>
> ROMANS 15:4

FOR ME THE OLD Testament is almost always a struggle. The more I read it, the more I have sympathy with Richard Dawkins arguments in *The God Delusion*. I then repeat to myself the response to Dawkins voiced by many, "I don't believe in a God like that either." So reading the Old Testament is more often than not an exercise in confirming what I don't believe, rather than supporting what I do.

St Paul in his letter to the Romans offers some very practical advice that is as relevant today as it was when it was written. Our emphasis, based on skeptical disbelief would be different from his, but his words carry weight. Yes, "The scriptures written long ago" can indeed instruct and encourage us, and they may indeed help us to "maintain our hope", but for what? Paul was looking to the Second Coming. We (or at least those who think like I do) are looking for a better world, which may be a "second coming" in another guise. We need all the help and encouragement we can get to persevere with that hope, and some of this can indeed be found in the Old Testament (as well as the New), albeit with some reinterpretation.

Isaiah prophesies the arrival of someone with outstanding qualities. He will usher in a new world order where the normal behaviour of the animal kingdom (and by association all creatures, including human beings) will be turned on its head. The words are familiar, but the images of the wolf lying down with the lamb, and children playing among snakes, are still startling and shocking.

The pictures are also romantic and seductive, but do I believe them? I may hope for a new and perfect world, but my cynicism about human nature and the record of history suggests that we are a very long way from achieving it. Yet I have a sense that life would be better, if, as Isaiah goes on to say

> *There will be neither hurt nor harm in all my holy mountain; for the land and sea will be filled with knowledge of the Lord, as the waters cover the sea.* —Isaiah 11:9

No matter how exotic the images, looking beyond the metaphor the only way I can make this relevant to me is to question how I could make this happen. Isaiah gives some guidance. He cites the characteristics and qualities that will later be identified in Christ as a response to that prophecy. I need to ask whether they are qualities that could change the world.

The Bible has numerous such lists of virtuous behaviour and it is easy to dismiss them as desirable but unattainable pinnacles of goodness. We should at least begin to think constructively about what they mean to us. How do I demonstrate the behaviours listed by Isaiah?

Isaiah offers them in balancing pairs, and it is easy to ignore the power of their juxtaposition in the flow of reading: *wisdom and understanding; counsel and power; knowledge and fear of the Lord*. We need to ask ourselves some questions about each pair.

Is our *wisdom,* born of education and experience, used in a creative and productive way? Is our wisdom matched by our ability to understand those who do not see the world as we do? All too often our arrogant convictions born of past experience ignore where the people we are working with or talking to are coming from, setting up at best apathy and at worst resentment and rejection. Do we have the wisdom to recognise the importance of the things that we struggle to understand?

Counsel and power go to the heart of two modes of behaviour. Do we exert our influence and authority through supportive behaviour, advice, and guidance, or do we assume that we have a right to be authoritarian and demanding, knowing all too well that is not how we would like to be treated?

Knowledge and fear of the Lord are more difficult to translate into modern thinking. My own interpretation is that we must be humble about what we know about life, because in the grand scheme of things, we know next to nothing. The little that we do know and understand has to go a long way if we are going to help the world to change using truth and justice as our absolute values.

Mahatma Gandhi famously said, "Be the change you wish to see in the world", and that for me is the only way we can make better things happen. No matter how pious or unfashionably virtuous it may sound, we need to find ways to demonstrate in ourselves what we think and hope the world should look like.

Third Sunday of Advent

Patience

Isaiah 35:1–10 James 5:7–10

Psalm 146:4–10 Matthew 11:2–11

Then the eyes of the blind will be opened, and the ears of the deaf unstopped. Then the lame will leap like deer, and the dumb shout aloud; for water will spring up in the wilderness and torrents flow in the desert. The mirage will become a pool, the thirsty land bubbling springs; instead of reeds and rushes, grass will grow in country where wolves have their lairs.

Isaiah 35:5–7

You must be patient my friends until the Lord comes. Consider: the farmer looking for the precious crop from his land can only wait in patience until the early and the late rains have fallen. You too must be patient and stout-hearted, for the coming of the Lord is near.

James 5:7–8

John, who was in prison, heard what Christ was doing and sent his own disciples to put this question to him: 'Are you the one who is to come, or are we to expect someone else?' Jesus answered, 'Go and report to John what you hear and see: the blind recover their sight, the lame walk, lepers are made clean, the deaf hear, the dead are raised to life, the poor are brought good news—and blessed are those who do not find me an obstacle to faith.'

Matthew 11:2–6

I WAS BROUGHT UP to believe that patience was indeed a virtue, but it was very difficult for me, as a child, to really understand why waiting for something without fuss or complaint was in itself a good thing.

The idea was made more palatable by the notion that "good things come to those who wait." For a child, waiting, particularly in the lead up to Christmas, with the belief that there would be good things at the end, with happy memories to prove it, made a lot of sense.

I have learned, as we all do, that being patient does not always bring good things, but it does have many virtues. It allows time for thought, deepens understanding, builds value, increases appreciation, and heightens gratitude.

Modern life however has moved in a different direction. We can go places faster, take only minutes to search for goods, services or entertainment on-line, buy things quicker, borrow money almost instantly, have things delivered within hours, so why wait? If you can afford it, need it, want it, why not have it now?

We are so used to this, and so accustomed to bemoaning an instant gratification mentality and 'want-it-now" culture, that even to talk about it seems trite and smug, as if we never, ever displayed any of those characteristics ourselves. Have we ever seized the moral high ground because we were prepared to wait for something for no other reason than we had been brought up to believe that was a good thing to do? Mentally, perhaps, but not publicly. To most people who know us, if not society as a whole, such a position would be laughably pointless.

Sometimes we have to be patient because there is no other way to behave. This is the argument in the letter of James, who is thought to have been the brother of Jesus. He makes the very simple point that in many activities and endeavours (like farming) once we have done all we can do by way of preparation, investment of time, money and care, all we can do is wait for good results to come. James was confident in the validity of his analogy because of his confident belief in the second coming. Many of us would have difficulty sharing that confidence.

Patience becomes difficult, when what we want is itself difficult, unattainable for now, complex in achievement and delivery, or requires us to take many personal steps before fulfilment can be achieved. Getting things is easy, getting the things that matter is difficult and requires patience. Finding where, and how, and in what form, and when the Christian faith will make sense to me is patience of that kind. It is hard to be patient if you are not sure what you are waiting for.

We have already talked about expectation and anticipation in relation to Advent, both of which require large measures of patience if they are not to degenerate into dispirited frustration. These readings leap forward and take us beyond the birth of Christ to his adult ministry. Here was evidence of the patience of centuries, built on Old Testament prophesies, being rewarded. Life was going to change, and at that time the evidence was clear.

Isaiah gives us another prophesy of the new world order, this time with changes that will make a tangible difference to every human being. This is what people were patiently waiting for. It is therefore not surprising that Jesus was tetchy with the questions asked by John the Baptist's followers. It is as if he is saying "You have been waiting for this for literally ages, and you don't recognise when it happens, even when nothing like it has happened before."

The passage from Matthew ends with a deeply challenging saying: *Blessed are those who do not find me an obstacle to faith*. For me this means be prepared to recognise the truth in the unexpected things I may discover, even if they contradict previously held views or beliefs. Be open-minded. Don't let doubts about circumstances, personal prejudice, or second guessing get in the way of something, however intangible, that may be or value. Don't let the messenger get in the way of the message.

It is important for me in the third chapter of this book to think about this. This is an exploration, and one that starts with much doubt and prejudice. I am impatient to find answers, but impatience is counter-productive.

Patience will produce its own rewards, and I must not let the things that I find meaningful stand in the way of the meaning for which I am searching.

Fourth Sunday of Advent
Believing the Unbelievable

Isaiah 7:10–16 Romans 1:1–7
Psalm 80:1–8, 18–20 Matthew 1:18–25

This gospel God announced beforehand in sacred scriptures through his prophets. It is about his Son: on the human level he was a descendant of David, but on the level of the spirit—the Holy Spirit—he was proclaimed Son of God by an act of power that raised him from the dead: it is about Jesus Christ our Lord.

Romans 1:2–4

This is how the birth of Jesus came about. His mother Mary was betrothed to Joseph; before their marriage she found she was going to have a child. Being a man of principle, and at the same time wanting to save her from exposure, Joseph made up his mind to have the marriage contract quietly set aside.

Matthew 1:18–19

He had resolved on this, when an angel of the Lord appeared to him in a dream and said, 'Joseph, son of David, do not be afraid to take Mary home with you to be your wife. It is through the Holy Spirit that she has conceived. She will bear a son; and you shall give him the name Jesus, for he will save his people from their sins.'

Matthew 1:20–21

BELIEVING THE UNBELIEVABLE

IN THE READING FROM Matthew for the Third Sunday of Advent Jesus said *"Blessed are those who do not find me an obstacle to faith."* My mother, who recently celebrated her 100th birthday, was the daughter of a Methodist Minister, and married to a Methodist Minister, so the church has always been deeply part of her life. In her later years she became more and more intolerant of traditional thinking and talking about Christianity, summed up in her memorable statement, "I've no time for Jesus, but a lot of time for God." Jesus for her was indeed an obstacle to her faith.

The whole Christmas story for many people, including me, has the same effect. Positive responses quickly turn into dubious negatives. On one level I can understand the importance of the birth of Jesus in the Christian context, both symbolically and actually. The more I think about it, however, the more difficult it becomes.

I am challenged to wonder about the meaning of Old Testament prophesies and whether this was a realisation of them. I am more willing to believe that in the New Testament there is a literary shoe-horning of events to fit pious expectation.

I have great difficulty with the extraordinary concept, or should that be conceit, of the name "Son of God." We read that so often, it is such an integral part of the weft and warp of Christian thinking and teaching, and repetition breeds blind acceptance. But how can it be?

I am not talking about whether a virgin birth is possible, and what *"It is through the Holy Spirit that she has conceived"* really means. For me that goes beyond thought, and does not really matter. We can take it at face value if we so wish, or reject it as literary licence and imaginative storytelling if that is more palatable. In either case we are left with the fact of a birth. So far so good.

I struggle with the idea of an unknowable God causing (if you can use such a word for God) this to happen, then, with those people, for a purpose—saving people from their sins—that is based on an arcane concept of the Fall of Man and the resulting sinfulness of everyone. I am more than willing to admit that my understanding of the deeper meaning may be faulty or inadequate, but "from the pew" this is the presenting story and rationale. So far so not very good at all.

Paul has no difficulty with any of this. In his letter to the Romans above he confidently sets out the stall of his belief. He knows who and what he is talking about it. His confidence, repeated by many from then until now is infectious. If you say it firmly, without equivocation or self-doubt, people will believe, even if they don't understand you. Can you believe without understanding? I'm not sure. Some would argue that is what faith is. That's where I struggle.

In the middle of all this is a huge reality check, so often forgotten in the fog of exegesis, and obscured by the happy lights of Christmas celebrations. Joseph was not a happy man. His story brings us all down to earth. He was a father-to-be, discovering that his wife was about to have a baby that was not his, yet principled and caring enough (we are told) to save her from embarrassment by contemplating a secret divorce. It is always dangerous to interpret custom and practice two thousand years ago via the mores of today, but cynics would argue that such an action would save him from embarrassment rather than her.

Joseph certainly had a mixed response to the situation and mixed motives in trying to resolve it. He is one of us. He may well have ground his teeth and muttered in dark corners, but according to the story, he did not fly off the handle. Then he has a dream, and, you might say, the rest is history. Somehow he gets, or is given, another way of looking at and understanding his predicament, which he accepts, believing the unbelievable.

Soon Joseph disappears from the story of Jesus' life altogether, and is all too easily forgotten. He deserves more attention. He clearly loved his wife, and she him. He felt betrayed, perplexed, disbelieving, angry, cheated and a fool, yet he listened to some inner voice that suggested to him there was more here than met the eye, and good may come of it, but he had no real idea of that good might be. He responded to his inner calling, and good did come of it, but not without many trials and tribulations on the way. Is he a role model for us all?

Christmas Day

Trappings, Traditions and Words

Isaiah 52:7–10   Hebrews 1:1–4
Psalm 98   John 1:1–14

Let the sea resound and everything in it, the world and those who dwell there. Let the rivers clap their hands, let the mountains sing aloud together before the Lord; for he comes to judge the earth. He will judge the world with justice and the peoples with equity.

PSALM 98:7–9

He is the radiance of God's glory, the stamp of God's very being, and he sustains the universe by his word of power. When he had brought about purification of sins, he took his seat at the right hand of God's Majesty on high, raised as far above the angels as the title he has inherited is superior to theirs.

HEBREWS 1:3–4

In the beginning the Word already was. The Word was in God's presence, and what God was, the Word was. He was with God at the beginning, and through him all things came to be; without him no created thing came into being. In him was life, and that life was the light of mankind. The light shines in the darkness, and the darkness has never mastered it.

JOHN 1:1–5

CHRISTMAS HAS COME. THE waiting is over. The decorations have been up for weeks. The presents bought and wrapped. The stockings and the turkey stuffed. The children incandescent with excitement. The relatives are putting their best face on being with each other. The anxieties about the day itself quickly evaporate in a reasonable display of goodwill to all men. Then, as I get older, there is that nagging sadness, a niggling sense of anti-climax, a surreptitious questioning whether it was all worth it, a longing for the unfettered excitement of childhood, with that memory of presents unwrapped and not even played with yet.

Church, at Christmas, particularly Midnight Mass, has a feeling all its own. There is a comforting familiarity about carols, readings and prayers, a warm benevolence towards others, and a slightly embarrassed admission that 'this is what Christmas is all about - if only I had time to think about it'. The trappings and traditions of Christmas are what we look forward to, savour, remember, and paste into our mental family scrapbooks. The festivities seem to take for ever to arrive, with the build-up starting in October, if not earlier, and then they are over in a flash. Life moves on for another year, until next year. We don't have time to really think about Christmas.

The stories and the sentiment get in the way. We can all cope with Mary, Joseph, the Baby, the Stable, the Shepherds, the Angels, and in due course the Wise Men. They are in our blood, even if we have no time for anything religious, and never darken the doors of a church. It is the enormity of it all that is more difficult to handle.

That is what struck me most in the three sets of verses above from the Psalms, Hebrews, and John. Here we have people, struggling to find language to describe, or at least convey, their feelings about God, his purpose, and who this baby, described as the Son of God really was. It's heady stuff. The Psalmist, as is often the case, takes us into the poetic realms of anthropomorphic nature, with images that are breath-taking in their imagination, if we give the words a chance to sink in: rivers clapping, mountains singing, and the sea and sea-creatures making a loud noise. The writer of the Letter to Hebrews reminds us of who Christ really is, using language that we understand because we know the meaning of every word, but whose deeper meaning we struggle with. What is "God's glory" or "his very being" or "his word of power"? While we can accept (to a degree) what he is telling us about Christ's overall importance in the eternal scheme of things, can we really take seriously his description of a celestial hierarchy?

Then we come to John's Gospel, with some of the most moving yet obscure words in the whole of the New Testament, which for me set up profound trains of thought. Here are words that take us beyond words because they are just hinting at meaning. It is for us, for me, to interpret and explore them to see where they go.

Paradoxically words are the problem, if not the obstacles, to my thinking about the Christian faith and my ability to articulate my beliefs. I am sure I am not alone in this. At one level we can "tell the stories" with ease. That is what I find so frustrating about some of the preaching from the pulpit that I hear. I don't need explanations and interpretations that are mere reiterations, in less resounding words, of what has been read to us from the Bible that day. I don't need interpretations that beg questions by using the very words that make understanding difficult. Look again at the first line of the passage from Hebrews above. That's Bible language, and church language, it's not my language.

I recognise the inadequacy of language to even begin to explain, interpret, or demystify things that are inexplicable and mysterious. I still want to be taken down a path of words that will bring me a few steps closer to finding how these extraordinary Biblical words and images might mean something to me. May be this is asking for the impossible. Simplification, dumbing down, or passionate re-exposition are as bad as talking-up, philological analysis, or historical contextualisation. The words will just do what words do, miss the point, because the point is personal.

Christmas Day could not be more personal. Presents, people, food, drink, children, babies, family stories, family feuds, experiences that become the stuff of family legend, traditions that we later fondly replicate or equally fondly discard. For the lonely and destitute it is a time of acute unhappiness, exacerbated by the unfettered encouragements to have a good time from the commercial world. For the majority of us, it is indeed a good and happy time. At the back of our minds we will recall what it's all about, with vague recollections that pagan mid-winter festivals were in some way hijacked by Christianity. Does that really matter when we can have another slice of turkey, another glass of wine? This is not a one day event. A historical birth was the start of events that the rest of the Christian year celebrates. If the birth is going to mean anything to me, the words that surround it have to be the start of some new thinking.

First Sunday of Christmas
Testing Times

Isaiah 63:7–9   Hebrews 2:10–18
Psalm 148   Matthew 2:13–23

Praise the Lord from the earth, you sea monsters and ocean depths; fire and hail, snow and ice, gales of wind that obey his voice; all mountains and hills; all fruit trees and cedars; wild animals and cattle, creeping creatures and winged birds.

Psalm 148:7–10

He had to be made like his brothers in every way, so that he might be merciful and faithful as their high priest before God, to make expiation for the sins of the people. Because he himself has passed through the test of suffering, he is able to help those who are in the midst of their test.

Hebrews: 2:17–18

An angel of the Lord appeared to Joseph in a dream, and said, 'Get up, take the child and his mother, and escape with them to Egypt, and stay there until I tell you; for Herod is going to search for the child and kill him.' So Joseph got up, took mother and child by night, and sought refuge with them in Egypt, where he stayed until Herod's death.

Matthew 2:13–15

If Christmas Day was a time out from the harsh realities of the world, the readings for the next Sunday remind us that they have not gone away.

Herod, victim of his own insecurities, embarks on a concentrated massacre of all boys under two. To escape this, within days of Mary giving birth, Joseph sets off with mother and child on a journey of some fifty to one hundred miles across the border into Egypt.

All this makes a grim but gripping story that is easy to imagine. Bloodthirsty soldiers roaming the countryside. Terrified parents, begging for mercy and receiving none. A night escape by Joseph and Mary who are terrified of discovery. Temporary security in a foreign country. It is a story full of pain and suffering, irrational anger, murder, mayhem, hardship, worry and insecurity. Testing times.

It is intellectually testing to cope with all the contrasting messages in the passages above, and I wonder what I am to make of it all. All I know is that this is the start of the real struggle to make sense of the life and the message of the man who is now, in the story, in his mother's arms, travelling to escape death. We can reasonably assume that Joseph and Mary were equally perplexed. They must have been relieved that the birth was now over, despite the uncomfortable and unconventional surroundings, amazed at the visitors and gifts they had received, and horrified that this birth appeared to have precipitated royal wrath and massacre.

The Psalmist praising God as the maker and master of all things, encourages all nature to do the same because he is coming "to judge the earth . . . with justice . . . and equity." It is easy to enjoy the poetry, and make allowances for a different world view, but do I read this as a pious hope, or a prophesy which Christ in some way fulfils? If so, how? Or do I read this as an ironic contrast to Matthew's story—clapping rivers, and singing mountains offering an antidote to child killing? How could the former occupy the same poetic world as the latter?

The passage from Hebrews takes us further into the intellectual wilderness. Written much closer to the real events of Christ's life, we have moved away from judgement, we are now talking about special pleading and atonement "for the sins of the people." This is of course a constant theme throughout the New Testament, but for me repetition does not make it any easier to understand.

If one of the central tenets of the Christian faith is that "Christ died for our sins", why is there a tacit acceptance that we all understand what the means, and presumably feel better for it? Why do I need him to do that?

Why does God need him to do that? Does the transformation of the vengeful God of the Old Testament into the loving God of the New Testament have any importance outside Biblical literary and historical analysis? How can an event two thousand years ago make any difference to me now? The questions keep on coming. The answer remain elusive. Yet we have an answer of sorts.

To explore this answer, I have to accept for the moment (because if I don't I get nowhere) that Christ's birth, life and death have a meaning for us all today, and that thinking about him is a positive force for good in our lives, no matter how many questions this begs. Do I need to act as if I have faith so that faith will be given to me?

The answer lies in the same passage from Hebrews. The writer tells his readers then and now that because Christ was tested by his suffering, he can help those who are facing tests of their own. His experience means that he can empathise with us and support us in our hours of need. We know, and will explore further at Easter, that Christ struggled to understand why he had to suffer pain and humiliation, misunderstanding and rejection, clear evidence of his humanity. So he is on our wavelength.

He believed in and at the end, that his testing was for a purpose. A purpose that he might not understand but accepted. The passage from Hebrews encourages us to believe the same. Our intellectual testing and suffering is a path to understanding. We may be unclear what we are trying to understand, and why it is important, but we live in hope that will become clear in due course.

In the midst of all this uncertainty, there is one certainty. The only way I can understand what it means is to go through it. Putting difficult things to the back of my mind because thinking about them is difficult and painful is not the answer, and never will be.

Second Sunday of Christmas
Grace, Truth and Rejection

Jeremiah 31:7–14 Ephesians 1:3–14
Psalm 147:13–20 John 1:10–18

He showers down snow, white as wool, and sprinkles hoar frost like ashes; he scatters crystals of ice like crumbs; he sends the cold, and the water stands frozen; he utters his word, and the ice is melted; he makes the wind blow and the water flows again.

Psalm 147:16–18

He was in the world; but the world, though it owed its being to him, did not recognise him. He came to his own, and his own people would not accept him.

John 1:10–11

So the Word became flesh; he made his home among us, and we saw his glory, such glory as befits the Father's only Son, full of grace and truth.

John 1:14

Reading these passages I was struck by the extraordinary contradictions of the Christian faith which are both part of its strength and a stumbling block for many, myself included. Those with a firm belief appear to be able to take these in their stride, or ignore them as too difficult to handle. The confidence that enables believers to be able to say "I may not understand all this now, but it will all come clear in the end" is admirable, but unhelpful to those for whom struggling to understand is the natural way to approach life's perplexities.

First of all we have wonderfully poetic verses from the Psalms extolling the powers of a creator God who, in the psalmist's view, controls the weather. We may enjoy or ridicule the picture the psalmist paints, but he reminds us that while we may, to some degree at least, understand the weather, its sheer power, beauty, and variety are truly awe-inspiring. To that extent we are one with the psalmist. We may however have different views on cause and effect. That then is the Old Testament view of God.

When we come to the New Testament and we find John offering a precise and concise summary of the life of Christ, the Son of God. The creator of the world was now walking in it, and nobody recognised him. This Gospel was probably written a century after the birth of Christ. Time has smoothed over doubts and uncertainties. Beliefs that were once fanciful are now entrenched. Interpretations are built on personal experience, new thinking, and links to earlier writing. John speaks allusively yet confidently. He extrapolates the events which lasted only a very short time in Palestine some sixty or seventy years earlier to the world as a whole. For him the rejection of the Son of God "by the world" must have seemed an astonishing and disastrous error, which he must address.

Not everyone, however, rejected Christ, and John (speaking as if he was there, but probably drawing on the memories of those who were) says "we saw his glory, such glory as befits the Father's only Son, full of grace and truth." There were those who recognised, or were helped to recognise, Christ's true nature. They came to understand his relationship with God, exemplified in the two core characteristics of grace and truth.

For me John's words help to convince me that Christ's birth and life on earth proved that God works in and through people, and not by managing the weather. Meeting a person who has grace and embodies truth truly brings God down to earth. I find it helpful to think of grace as human behaviour at its best, embodying everything that we would want to display in ourselves and therefore would wish to emulate. To disentangle grace into many sub-characteristics, into a virtuous and almost endless string of words such as gentleness, courtesy, caring, understanding, charm, loving and lovableness may explain in part but ultimately destroy the all-embracing nature of grace.

The OCD defines grace as "the free and unearned favour of God." I am not sure that I understand that. I do believe that grace expresses the essence of what God is in us (words are failing me here, but that's as close as I can get). If God's creation and our part in it makes any sense, it can only be that he has endowed us with the best (in our terms) of what he (in his terms) has to give.

John does not identify grace alone, but couples it with truth and sees the two together as the key characteristics of Christ. This for me, makes the description even more powerful. Not only do we have someone who has shown in his life, behaviour and personality the best humanity can aspire to, but he is also full of truth. Not only is he personally morally impeccable and unimpeachable, and he has a unique ability to explain the truth about life and death because of his closeness to God. This relationship also suggests that he has a true and complete understanding of everything, and as the Psalmist says, he does know how the snow falls, water freezes, and the winds blow. Thus he truly brings together the two extremes of a creator god and his struggling creation.

The message from John is not just about grace and truth. It is also about rejection, one of the most common and painful aspects of human behaviour. Like it or not, we reject what we don't understand, we reject what we don't like, we reject things that seem difficult in favour of something easier, we reject (though our liberal thoughts say otherwise) those who are different from us, we reject people or situations that make us think painfully about ourselves and our place in the world. If Christ came again, today, we would fail to understand him, and we would reject him, again. It is unlikely that we would kill him, but reject him we would.

So for me, the convincing evidence of Christ's importance, both as man and Son of God (accepting that for the moment as a shorthand for a mysterious, close relationship with God) is not just that he was full grace and truth, but that he was rejected for that very reason. Human nature having evolved as it has done, and being what is, then and now, we could not and cannot understand his godliness which is more threatening than healing. Where does that leave us? Where does it leave me?

The Epiphany
Birth and Death

Isaiah 60:1–6   Ephesians 3:1–12

Psalm 72   Matthew 2:1–12

Jesus was born in Bethlehem in Judaea during the reign of Herod. After his birth astrologers from the east arrived in Jerusalem, asking, 'Where is the new-born king of the Jews? We observed the rising of his star, and we have come to pay him homage.'

MATTHEW 2:1–2

'Go and make a careful search for the child and when you have found him, bring me word so that I may go myself and pay him homage'

MATTHEW 2:8

Entering the house they saw the child with Mary his mother and bowed low in homage to him; they opened their treasure chests and presented gifts to him: gold, frankincense, and myrrh. Then they returned to their own country by another route, for they had been warned in a dream not to go back to Herod.

MATTHEW 2:11–12

THE EPIPHANY READINGS ARE full of "riches", a word we do not use very much today. We live in a more prosaic age where wealth is money in the bank, diamonds on the fingers, cars in the drive, houses across the world, private jets, and couture clothes. How dull all that sounds against "treasure chests", which echo that passage from Isaiah who talks about "sea-borne riches", "the wealth of nations" and "camels laden with gold and frankincense" coming to a real and metaphorical new Jerusalem.

The riches that Matthew describes are far from prosaic. They are appropriate gifts to be offered to a king, but they have a wider significance. Gold was as important then as it is now, and a traditional royal gift. Frankincense as the name suggests was associated with prayer and connections to God. Myrrh was used for embalming bodies and for incense at funeral ceremonies. The gifts therefore encapsulate the nature of the new born child, his connection with God, and look forward to the inevitability of his death.

The mystery and the magic deepens with the very nature of the Three Kings, or Wise Men or as we are accustomed to call them. Were they indeed kings, or were they astrologers as the Revised English Bible translation suggests. They are also called Magi which contains hints of a pagan priesthood and sorcery. So is there an even deeper suggestion here that other magical forces in the world were now showing honour and respect to the Son of God.

As with so much in the Christmas story, the picture is attractive and romantic. The carols that celebrate the event are well known. The symbolism is familiar. Yet the meaning is obscure. That however may be the point of the whole story. The Three Wise Men, whoever they might have been, had come a long way, guided in some celestial way to reach their unexpected destination safely, yet they were no clearer than we are why they had come. We can unpack the symbolism, make the connections with earlier stories, and speculate about the people involved in the story, but we are really none the wiser.

Meanwhile, Herod, as we have already seen, was feeling threatened and in high dudgeon that anyone should suggest that a child had been born with aspirations to kingship. In the middle of the romanticism and sentiment of the birth, we have a man in a temper intent on murder, not just of one male child, but all male children in his kingdom. We could not ask for a more extreme example of humanity at its worst in the middle of humanity at its seeming best.

The story does Herod no favours. He is sly and dissembling, telling the Three Wise Men that he would like to visit this extraordinary child and pay his respects, yet planning his death. To stretch word association to its limits, we are tempted to say "That's rich."

The Christmas story is challenging because it is so well known that it becomes a fact in our minds. We have imagined the scene, aided by Fra Angelico, Piero della Francesca, Botticelli, Michelangelo, Rubens, El Greco, and hundreds of other artists. We have taken part in the Nativity plays, heard the Biblical accounts, and sung the carols countless times. I see it clearly, but I do not understand it.

Who do I identify with? A stroppy innkeeper, with a busy inn to run and no time for a young women about to give birth knocking on his door: busiest night of the year; customers to attend to; use the stable. Shepherds who are amazed, excited, spellbound with no idea what's really happening, but a sense that it is important. "Wise men" (but where lies their wisdom?) who are equally excited, equally mystified. T. S Eliot in *The Journey of the Magi* suggests that this was the moment when their world view changed, leaving them puzzled and dissatisfied with their earlier beliefs. Is it the same for me?

Satiated by Christmas saccharine the one thing that gives the whole story a painful and challenging edge for me is that no one really knew what was going on, and the only thing that would make sense of it would be the death of the child that had just been born. A child who had narrowly escaped death at the hands of Herod, but was now being offered a gift that reminds his parents, and us, that this story will end in a painful and unnatural death.

"Epiphany" means an astonishing, amazing, sometimes supernatural, revelation. In this case of course it is the revelation of the infant Christ to the Three Wise Men. The festival of Epiphany, on 6 January, is also traditionally the last day of Christmas. The twelve days of feasting and jollity are now coming to an end, and normal life resumes. As the Wise Men set off home "by another route" did they feel, as T.S Eliot suggests that normal life had resumed, but it had somehow changed?

Christ's birth is fact, though the circumstances and attendant characters may be fanciful. If the facts of Christ's birth, life, and death are going to mean anything to me, then the Wise Men will have to be my role model. I too may have to change my world view, and find another route, mindful that nothing is as certain as how the story ends.

The Baptism of Christ
(First Sunday of Epiphany)

Start of Life's Work

Isaiah 42:1–9   Acts 10:34–43

Psalm 29   Matthew 3:13–end

Here is my servant, whom I uphold, my chosen one, in whom I take delight! I have put my spirit on him; he will establish justice among the nations. He will not shout or raise his voice, or make himself heard in the street. He will not break a crushed reed or snuff out a smouldering wick; unfailingly he will establish justice. He will never falter or be crushed until he sees justice on earth, while coasts and islands await his teaching.

Isaiah 42:1–4

Then Jesus arrived at the Jordan from Galilee, and came to John to be baptized by him. John tried to dissuade him, 'Do you come to me?' he said. 'It is I who need to be baptized by you.' Jesus replied, 'Let it be so for the present; it is right for us to do all that God requires.' Then John allowed him to come.

Matthew 3:13–15

No sooner had Jesus been baptized and come up out the water than the heavens opened and he saw the Spirit of God descending like a dove to alight on him. And there came a voice from heaven saying, 'This is my beloved son, in whom I take delight.'

Matthew 3:16–17

Matthew uses Isaiah's words to describe the baptism of Jesus by John. We can assume that Matthew's readers would recognise the cross-reference, understand the additional meaning that Isaiah's words add to his account, and appreciate what in their eyes was the fulfilment of an Old Testament prophesy.

Distanced by a couple of thousand years, I can recognise the allusions and echoes, and enjoy the added weight and mystery that comes from the juxtaposition of these two passages, but I am still puzzled.

Historians have great confidence that Christ's baptism was an actual event, and it is commonly regarded as the event that marks the start of Christ's public ministry. So far so good, but why did he need to be baptised at all? If we understand baptism as a symbolic representation of our entry into, or reception by, the Christian church, how do we interpret the baptism of the man without whom there would be no church? If we are comfortable (which I am not) with a symbolism of water and a washing away of sins, how does that relate to a man who many regard as "without sin"?

Even John the Baptist is perplexed. He feels the situation should be reversed with Christ baptising him, which is easy to understand. Christ responds with a simply statement that has (for me) great significance. *"Let it be so for the present; it is right for us to do all that God requires."* Translations in various Bible versions vary considerably, and are generally for more obscure than this. Here we have Jesus being sensitive and pragmatic. My interpretation is that he does not want anything at this stage in his life to suggest that he is in any way different from those around him, nor did he want to claim special privileges (as the Son of God) in advance of his own preaching ministry when he would explain who he was to a wide audience.

This low key approach is convincing and admirable in its humility. The next part of the story however takes the whole event literally to another dimension. Two men, quietly agree a way forward, and the baptism takes place. Then imagination runs riot and we have the heavens opening, the Spirit of God descending like a dove, and a booming (we assume) voice telling the world exactly who Jesus was. So much for low key.

It is as if Matthew, and the other Gospel writers, needed this kind of embellishment to confirm and enhance the importance of the story, both in the way they tell it, and the links back to Isaiah, which give it added relevance. Poetic language, images of doves descending, voices from Heaven are all very well, but for me they obscure, or at least distract attention from the simpler, quieter events and thoughts which contain the heart of this story.

How touching and powerful it is when someone with enormous authority humbly puts this on one side to be involved in a 'ritual', or we might say 'programme of activity' organised by someone else. This action recognises that respect for the integrity of a person carries far more weight than obedience to his or her position.

The passage from Isaiah emphasises the softer characteristics which are completely at odds with the voice from heaven image in Matthew. This is an encouragement to us all to think about a model of behaviour that could and should change the world. I read 'justice' in the widest possible sense. It embraces the operation of the law, but that is secondary to the concept of equality and fair treatment for all.

Isaiah offers us convincing guidance that 'justice' is best achieved not by shouting in the street, demagogy, and rabble-rousing, but by quiet determination. He makes a particular and telling reference to the "crushed reed" and "smouldering wick", evocative images that remind us that we have a duty of care to support those who are struggling in their efforts to create a just world. The fact that they are faltering does not mean that they have no contribution to make and therefore should be rejected or ignored. Quite the contrary. It is for us to support them to enhance and encourage what they are trying to do.

Using Isaiah's words to interpret Jesus' purpose we are led to believe that he, unlike us, will not "falter or be crushed until he sees justice on earth" and this is what he has been sent to tell the world. He therefore becomes a role model for us all.

The delight or pleasure a father has in his child's achievements and potential is something with which we can all identify. Baptism is a symbolic start of a life journey to realise that potential for us all. This will be achieved by the quiet pursuit of what we believe is right, even though we will often lack enthusiasm and feel crushed.

Second Sunday of Epiphany

Conundrums of Calling

Isaiah 49:1–7   I Corinthians 1:1–9
Psalm 40:1–12   John 1:29–42

Then I said, 'Here I am,' as is prescribed for me in a written scroll. God, my desire is to do your will; your law is in my heart.

Psalm 40:7–8

There is indeed no single gift you lack, while you wait expectantly for our Lord Jesus Christ to reveal himself. He will keep you firm to the end, without reproach on the day of our Lord Jesus. It is God himself who called you to share in the life of his Son Jesus Christ our Lord; and God keeps faith.

1 Corinthians 1:7–9

The next day again, John was standing with two of his disciples when Jesus passed by. John looked towards him and said, "There is the Lamb of God!" When the two disciples heard what he said, they followed Jesus.

John 1:35–37

ARE WE CALLED TO believe, or do we believe that we are called?

This kind of perplexity is captured well in the three passages above, and is a problem that is a real struggle for me. I listen with skepticism to people who say with unwavering conviction that they believe God is calling them to do something. I am skeptical because I do not share their strength of faith and belief, and I am uncharitable enough to think that they may be deluding themselves. Is my attitude reasonable and rational, or biased and bigoted?

I have personal experience of people who "responded to God's call" to do something that all the evidence suggested was unnecessary or unwanted. In one particular case it was to go to Biafra towards the end of the Nigerian Civil War to offer medical help at a time when all the reports said that the help needed was of an entirely different kind—food and post-conflict recovery.

I am sure that people will argue that I have no right to question or second guess God's call. My judgement of the situation may not be his. The outcome of the response may be entirely different from my prediction. God moves in a mysterious way. These are arguments that in my more generous and uncritical moments I am prepared to accept, but it leaves me with a nagging doubt about the specific nature of any call. Is it expressed by a sense of compulsion "I feel I must. . . .", "I have a feeling that I ought to. . . .", or is it something more vague and nebulous, "May be I should explore whether I could. . . .", "Sometime I wonder whether I might . . . "? Is there any correlation between the strength of the conviction and its realisation?

Thomas Merton in his famous prayer, captured this poignantly

> "My Lord God, I have no idea where I am going. I do not see the road ahead of me. I cannot know for certain where it will end. Nor do I really know myself, and the fact that I think that I am following your will does not mean that I am actually doing so."

Is this an antidote to conviction, or the very stuff of which real conviction is made?

The three passages above give us glimpses of different ways of thinking that are helpful in reaching an understanding of this conundrum.

Psalm 40 is a complex poem in which the psalmist's willingness to serve God is sandwiched between words of praise and thanks: *Lord my God, great things you have done; your wonder and your purpose are for our good*, and statements of all the good and worthy things the psalmist has done: *In the great assembly I have proclaimed what is right; I do no hold back my words*. Then a somewhat aggrieved cry that despite all this: *Misfortunes beyond counting press on me from all sides.* But in the middle he suggests that the call to which he responds with *'Here I am'* is somehow part of his destiny, *as is prescribed for me in a written scroll,* and an inevitable consequence of his beliefs and faith. So I am led to wonder whether our life is a call, and our calling our life.

Paul in his letter to Christians in Corinth suggests that God will give them the strength to continue the ministry to which they are called, and has already given them the gifts they need. Does this mean that our calling is determined by, or already lies in, the gifts and talents that we have? Are we ever "called" to do something for which we lack any aptitude, interest, or skill? Although it is counter-intuitive to believe that you can be champion jockey despite the fact that you can't ride and hate horses, there is nothing in life to suggest that an apparently bizarre ambition should not result in the discovery of a new skill or passion. The mystery of God is that he does work in a mysterious way.

Finally, we have the story of the calling of the first disciples. Two are mentioned here, one of whom was Andrew, Simon Peter's brother. They are called "disciples" of John, so clearly they were already close followers and believers in what he had to say. John had already talked at length about *"Among you, though you do not know him, stands the one who is to come after me. I am not worthy to unfasten the strap of his sandal."* His disciples were primed to expect someone else, but how would they recognise him? When John points out Jesus to them with the words *"There is the Lamb of God!"* they immediately respond. They were predisposed to a calling, they trusted the guidance they were given, and they responded to an enigmatic phrase that would have little meaning until they had heard at length what Jesus had to say.

I take heart from these readings. To me they suggest that we are predisposed for certain paths in life by our skills, talents, interests and aspirations, but we frequently need someone or some event to point us in the right direction, and this calling will be more powerful if we have to work hard to understand what it means. Working hard to follow a particular path makes it all worthwhile.

Third Sunday of Epiphany
Rhetoric and Reason

Isaiah 9:1–4 1 Corinthians 1:10–18
Psalm 27:1–11 Matthew 19:27–end

The people who walked in darkness have seen a great light; on those who lived in a land as dark as death a light has dawned.

Isaiah 9:2

Christ did not send me to baptize, but to proclaim the gospel; and to do it without recourse to the skills of rhetoric, lest the cross of Christ be robbed of its effect.

1 Corinthians 1:17

"Anyone who has left houses, or brothers or sisters, or father or mother, or children or land for the sake of my name will be repaid many times over, and gain eternal life. But many who are first will be last, and the last first."

Matthew 19:29–30

THESE THREE PASSAGES SEEM to contradict each other, and the words that are used to clarify difficult concepts serve only to make them more obscure.

Isaiah offers hope that somehow, somewhere everything will begin to make sense. Our mental darkness will be illuminated by the light of understanding. Jesus uses similar words to describe himself: "*I am the light of the world. No follower of mine shall walk in darkness; he shall have the light of life.*" (John 8:12) and it is easy to understand this in relation Christ's life and teaching. He brings, or brought, a new view of humanity, a new view of our obligations to each other, a new view of moral codes and diktats, a new view of the purpose of our lives, and a new view of the nature of death.

The difficulty is that we have to believe him, the New Testament would say "in him", for this to make sense. Much of it is contrary to our normal behaviour, and contrary to our understanding of the natural world. The light is shining in the dark corners of our mind, but are we any the wiser?

Christ's preaching, as recorded in the Gospels, contained a mixture of profound and world-changing phrases that were often difficult to understand until clarified by parables with a more homely appeal, and actions that did indeed speak louder than words. It is interesting to speculate the extent to which the accounts of Jesus' preaching are an accurate record. The parables were easily memorable and stood the test of time, but were his pregnant sayings conflated and given added weight by the disciples and those who came after them?

What is certain, is that Jesus was a very persuasive speaker, who was acutely aware of his audiences, and tailored what he had to say to suit them. He challenged priests with new interpretations of their own scripture. He saw through questions designed to trip him up and turned them back on his questioner. He helped people reach a view of the world that they recognised as making more sense than their current beliefs and practices, hidebound as these were by rules and regulations whose observance was supposed to determine virtue but in fact eroded humanity. He continually stretched his disciples with words that fired their imagination, and stretched their comprehension, so that they teetered on the edge of understanding, just as we do.

Paul in his letter to the Corinthians makes it clear that he is not going to use the "skills of rhetoric." In his eyes rhetoric has a bad name. Paul implies that it is a way of using language to persuade people to believe something against their better judgement, or to appeal to their emotions to win hearts rather than minds. He does not want anything to get in the way of the raw impact of Christ's crucifixion and all it stands for.

The difficulty for us, and Paul's readers, is that you had to be there. Repetition inures us to horrors, and the repeated cries "You've no idea how terrible it was" in the end leave us cold. Paul is a little ingenuous. His own experience and understanding, no matter how passionately voiced, are not themselves a guarantee that others will feel and believe as he does. We are now the 'others', and we need the skills of rhetoric, in the best sense, to open our hearts and our minds to what is being said.

Jesus' words, as reported by Matthew above, are a classic example of words that go beyond rhetoric. This is a powerful statement, made more so by the accumulating list of what and who has been left behind, and the antithesis of first and last at the end. Our hearts may be engaged, and the words are easily memorable, but what do they mean. The light may well be shining in the darkness, but we don't understand it. What does *"gain eternal life"* mean, and how do we make sense of *"the first will be last, and the last first"*? Other passages in the Gospels and the Epistles help us to understand these words, but on first hearing they are difficult.

I can understand that Jesus was teaching us in the pursuit of a better world the materially rich, the arrogant, the superior, those who assume status and put themselves first, will be overtaken by those who are more humble, caring, and are willing to serve rather than lord it over others. Service is more powerful than power itself.

I cannot get to grips with the concept of eternal life in any eschatological sense. I am not sure what I believe about death or life after it. If God makes any sense (which is itself a contradiction in terms) then anything is possible, and we may in some unimaginable way 'continue' after death. This makes more sense of our creation, than an incredibly short lifespan (in the context of the universe) of a mere century. Temporal analysis however makes no sense when we are talking about things eternal.

I am left with a belief that the best aspects of people, the best things in life, the best that we can create, the best that we can be, all these good things, will last longer than we do, and if emulated by others, there is no reason (if reason is what is needed) why they should not last for ever.

The Presentation of Christ in the Temple (Candlemas)

Struggling Thoughts

Malachi 3:1–5   Hebrews 2:14–end
Psalm 24   Luke 2:22–40

Who may go up the mountain of the Lord? Who may stand in his holy place? One who has clean hands and a pure heart, who has not set his mind on what is false or sworn deceitfully.

PSALM 24:3–4

I shall appear before you in court, quick to testify against sorcerers, adulterers, and perjurers, against those who cheat the hired labourer of his wages, who wrong the widow and the fatherless, who thrust the alien aside, and do not fear me, says the Lord of Hosts.

MALACHI 3:5

Simeon blessed them and said to Mary his mother, 'This child is destined to be a sign that will be rejected; and you too will be pierced to the heart. Many in Israel will stand or fall because of him; and so the secret thoughts of many will be laid bare.'

LUKE 2:34–35

IN LUKE'S ACCOUNT OF the birth of Christ, within the space of some twenty verses, we have the birth, the shepherds, and then a series of rituals as laid down by Jewish law and practice: circumcision and naming, Mary's purification after birth, and the presentation of Jesus in the temple with appropriate offerings. This is a fast-moving story that starts with extraordinary events, consolidates itself in a description of practices that establish who Jesus is and where he belongs, and then ends, in the passage above, when an old man, Simeon, casts a shadow over the events with his prophesy of pain and rejection, yet another mental burden for Mary.

Simeon's words then start an interesting train of thought. Nothing is perfect. The extraordinary revelations of Mary's pregnancy, the birth of Jesus itself, and the happiness of everything associated with what we now call Christmas, are all overshadowed by hints of death and pain. Simeon had been told that he would not die until he had seen *"the Lord's Messiah"*, and seeing Jesus in the temple meant that he died happy, but he sees pain to come, and his words are enigmatic.

"Many in Israel will stand or fall because of him" suggests to me that Simeon recognises that the impact of Christ's life and teaching will not be straightforward. The virtuous behaviour that the Psalmist advocates as the ticket of entry to the presence of God is not something that everyone can aspire to or achieve. In fact we all know how easy it is to become irritated by constant exhortations to the virtuous life, and the constant juxtaposition of evil and good. Some of us, some of the time, recognise the importance of doing right things to, with, by, and for others, though we may feel that "doing good" sounds too pious and holier-than-thou. We make an effort to stand by these principles, and stand up for what is right.

By contrast Malachi gives a list of "wrongs" that seems remarkably modern. *"Sorcerers, adulterers, and perjurers"* may not occupy our thoughts much, but low pay, exploitation, reductions in benefits, abuse in children's homes, lonely old age, and the treatment of immigrants, all contain any number of "wrongs" that we have an obligation to think about hard and long in the hope that we can find a way to improve them.

More often than not, however, we fail, or in Luke's words *"fall"* because the Christian life is a tough call. The higher the standard or example we are trying to follow, the further we fall when we fail. Failure can be understood only the context of what we are trying to achieve, and so in Simeon's words it is just as much *"because of him"* as is its virtuous opposite.

This is a constant mental battle for us all: what we want to do against what we ought to do; what we would like to do against what we need to do; what we should have said against what we did say; how we behaved on the spur of the moment, and how we might have behaved after a moment's thought.

Simeon understands all this. *"The secret thoughts of many will be laid bare"* seems on first reading to suggest an exposure of something bad, and a characteristic of those who "fall." For me it carries a much more powerful and helpful message if we understand *"secret thoughts"* as a simple description of what goes on in our minds. Of course our thoughts are secret, and just as well. We no more wish other people to know what we are thinking about them, than we wish to expose thoughts we have about life in general, hopes and uncertainties, fears and ambitions, loves and hates, beliefs and perplexities. The daily turmoil in our minds is indeed a headache.

Simeon is suggesting that Christ will have a unique insight into our minds and hearts. He is human and understands the human condition. He is facing the same turmoil himself, yet he recognises that this is the essential nature of God's creation. He knows, and will help us to know, that God sees more than we can ever see, and that whilst we struggle between opposing forces in our moral universe, God cares more about the struggle than the choice. Christ encourages us to lay bare our thoughts so that we admit our struggles, and by so doing we are helped to live our lives more fully.

We have all read about the moral strictures of earlier times, and we recall the things we were forbidden to do as we grew up, that now seem ridiculous and petty. Obeying rules set out in some arbitrary canon of behaviour based on misguided interpretations of Christian teaching must be the ultimate folly, and guarantee of failure.

If our "rules" hinder the enjoyment of life, and stunt personal and emotional growth, they are of no value and have little virtue. Yet so many of our mental struggles, often arising from our upbringing, are life limiting, not life enhancing. I believe that Simeon is telling us that Christ has come to help us see these rules for what they are, and to value the struggle to make sense of them as an essential part of the journey towards greater self-understanding and the realisation of our true potential. Laying bare our secret thoughts is a good thing.

Fourth Sunday before Lent
Salt and Spirit

Isaiah 58:1–9a   I Corinthians 2:1–12
Psalm 112:1–9   Matthew 5:13–20

Is not this the fast I require: to loose the fetters of injustice, to untie the knots of the yoke, and set free those who are oppressed, tearing off every yoke? Is it not sharing your food with the hungry, clothing the naked when you meet them, and never evading a duty to your kinsfolk?

ISAIAH 58:6–7

Scripture speaks of 'things beyond our seeing, things beyond our hearing, things beyond our imagining, all prepared by God for those who love him'; and these are what God has revealed to us through the Spirit. For the Spirit explores everything, even the depths of God's own nature. Who knows what a human being is but the human spirit within him? In the same way, only the Spirit of God knows what God is.

1 CORINTHIANS 2:9–11

"You are salt to the world. And if salt becomes tasteless, how is its saltiness to be restored? It is good for nothing but to be thrown away and trodden underfoot. You are light for all the world. A town that stands on a hill cannot be hidden. When a lamp is lit, it is not put under a meal-tub, but on the lampstand, where it gives light to

> *everyone in the house. Like the lamp, you must shed light among your fellows, so that when they see the good you do, they may give praise to your Father in heaven."*

MATTHEW 5:13–15

ISAIAH, IN THE VERSES preceding those above, writes about the hypocrisy of those who advocate fasting, but don't fast themselves, who fast but force their staff to work, who fast but end up arguing and fighting, and points out that fasting of that kind serves no religious or spiritual purpose of any kind. Fasting may not play any part in our lives today, but it is only a small stretch of the imagination to interpret "fasting" as meaning any religious practice or ritual.

The value of any religious observance is completely negated if our behaviour to others is contrary to and betrays the ethos and belief that we are celebrating or remembering. I wonder if we are as guilty of such hypocrisy today as people were when the Book of Isaiah was being written.

We don't have to look far for examples. Churches that are unwelcoming. Church committees which are characterised by in-fighting. Self-serving, inward-looking behaviour that excludes those who need the greatest help. A reluctance to look outwards as this may upset the status quo. A reluctance to accept different views of the world, and a suspicion of those who do. A polarisation between those who want things to continue as they always have, and those who want something new. A reluctance to hear other views and ideas. A smug complacent belief that virtue lies in regular attendance. Liturgy and ceremony that lacks heart. An embarrassment with 'sharing the peace' that reflects feelings that are anything but peaceful. In all a Church that fails in any number of ways. Above all it fails to practise what it preaches. In Matthew's words it is salt that has become tasteless. He makes it abundantly clear what needs to happen when this is the case.

Isaiah contrasts empty, 'tasteless' religious practise with behaviour that truly demonstrates what we would now call Christian behaviour. Following the preaching and teaching of Christ we need to find ways to build a just world, alleviate or remove mental and physical oppression, help those who are less fortunate than ourselves, and always seek ways to support our family. If more people tried to do this, in more places, more frequently they would indeed be a *"light to everyone in the house."*

That is one way of interpreting the words of Isaiah and the words of Matthew and relating them to life today, but is it all simply pious talk, whose "taste" is quickly obliterated by the realities of the everyday world? Do we pay lip-service to Biblical messages, and feel good doing so, but fail, as the church does, to make them a reality in our lives? Reluctantly I think we have to say yes, recognising however that there are always admirable exceptions to this rule which give us heart that it is possible to make a more positive response than a cynical recitation.

It is easy to become bogged down in negatives, to spend all our time talking about what is wrong, to point to what the church is not doing, to criticize those who are full of good intentions but fail to realize them, to focus on the tawdriness of everyday life and use this as an unsatisfactory and disheartening measure of what could be.

Paul in his letter to the Corinthians offers us an entirely different view, not of the temporal world, but of things spiritual that are beyond our imagination. By definition this is difficult to understand. It is even more difficult to relate this to pettiness among those organising the flower rota, and squabbles on the PCC.

I have great personal difficulty in understanding what the Spirit of God is. Many would say that if I could understand its true nature and purpose it would not be the Spirit of God. I cannot relate to the concept, nor respond to the imagery. The Spirit of God seems to have no purpose. If he is God by another name, why do we need another name? Do arguments of separateness and oneness, three in one, and one in three serve any purpose at all? And yet. And yet. We are dissecting abstractions, giving body to the spiritual, and using human measures to explain the immeasurable. Is it not more helpful to accept that we cannot understand who or what the Spirit of God is, and that Paul helps us down the path towards meaning?

Leaving all thoughts of God and Spirit on one side, I believe, with Paul, that there is something in us that makes us truly who we are. I can no more describe that medically than I can psychologically, but words like soul and spirit are pointing in the right direction. There is an essence in us that I believe is good, despite much evidence to the contrary. For me, this essence (to change metaphors, because that's all we have) is the salt that gives a new taste to life, and the lamp that gives new understanding of life.

The Third Sunday before Lent

Tough Talking

Deuteronomy 30:15–end   I Corinthians 3:1–9
Psalm 119:1–8   Matthew 5:21–37

I could not talk to you, my friends, as people who have the Spirit. I had to deal with you on the natural plane, as infants in Christ. I fed you milk, instead of solid food, for which you were not ready. Indeed, you are still not ready for it; you are still on the merely natural plane. Can you not see that as long as there is jealousy and strife among you, you are unspiritual, living on the purely human level?

I Corinthians 3:1–3

After all, what is Apollos? What is Paul? Simply God's agents in bringing you to faith. Each of us performed the task which the Lord assigned to him. I planted the seed, and Apollos watered it; but God made it grow. It is not the gardeners with their planting and watering who count, but God who makes it grow. Whether they plant or water, they work as a team, though each will get his own pay for his own labour. We are fellow-workers in God's service; and you are God's garden.

I Corinthians 3:5–9

If your right eye causes your downfall, tear it out and fling it away; it is better for you to lose one part of your body than for the whole of it to be thrown into hell. If your right hand causes your downfall, cut

TOUGH TALKING

> *it off and fling it away; it is better to lose one part of your body than for the whole of it to go to hell.*

MATTHEW 5:29–30

THERE IS SOME TOUGH talking in these passages. Paul harangues his readers in a manner that echoes Jesus haranguing his listeners. Both are expecting a great deal, and I wonder whether these words, without the sanctification of time, would be any more acceptable then than they are now. For me, there is nothing worse than being harangued from the pulpit. I really do not want to be told what to do by someone who holds the position of priest and teacher by a quirk of situation, education, and his or her view of vocation.

To be told that I am not ready for spiritual fare because my thoughts and behaviour are still bound up with human world, is both demeaning and insulting. I believe that we all need encouragement and understanding, not criticism. There may be many moments in our lives when we fail to live up to Christian ideals, but Christianity is a tough call. The fact that there are times when our lives are dominated by negative feelings for others, does not in itself mean that we cannot recognise, articulate and aspire to something better. To be told that we are spiritual failures saps the will and generates the very resentment that we are told is a symptom of that failure.

Jesus is even more outspoken. It is moments like this that remind me of Pier Paolo Pasolini's 1964 film *The Gospel according to St Matthew*. The landscape is barren and dusty. Jesus is a revolutionary in a hurry. When he talks he is brief and to the point. He does not suffer fools gladly. He wants to get his message across, and has little time in which to do it. His approach is uncompromising and his words harsh. In such a context this passage makes powerful metaphoric sense. Jesus wants to shock, and uses images of self-blinding and amputation that do just that.

The words are vivid, troubling and yet obscure. There is no literal way in which they make sense, but we immediately have a sense of what they mean. If there is something in our lives that is leading us astray, distracting us from our spiritual journey, or leading us down a morally reprehensible path, we need to cut it out of our lives. If we do not, the infection will spread, and eventually destroy us. Using Paul's imagery, this is solid food indeed, and very difficult to swallow.

It is natural to extend the metaphor of the body from the individual to the church, or even society, as a whole. Is Jesus really saying that if there are people who are leading us astray we need to get rid of them, kick them out, condemn, and reject them? It is possible to do this through the force of law, but in doing so we run the risk of being accused of injustice, discrimination, lack of understanding and lack of care, the very things that Jesus, and the Old Testament writers before him, are asking us to avoid at all costs.

Radical as he was, I do not believe that Jesus is advocating such a radical solution. The very fact that he uses such extreme imagery is a way of saying, this is something that we have to do, for the good of our souls (our essential self), for the good of our organisations, and for the good of society. The imperative command forces us to find a solution that achieves the same ends without bodily destruction.

Paul himself, in the verses that follow his words about baby food and unspiritual behaviour, offers us a new way of looking at this problem. We have to believe that *god's garden* is the world as we know it. We are all involved in making this a better place to live. We are all part of a continuous struggle to understand the 'higher', spiritual dimensions of life from a mundane, human perspective. Our language is inadequate, our behaviour inappropriate. We are distracted by some people with whom we come into contact, we are inspired by others. We make choices about who we are close to, and who not. There are of course people we do not want in our lives, but we recognise that this is a fact of life, not a death sentence. We are all working in this, and on this together, believing and hoping for the best. Without that faith in the fundamental goodness of life nothing will grow.

We are all *fellow workers in Gods service*, though it may at times be difficult to believe this. We will indeed be rewarded for the work and effort we put in because we will see things grow. We need to be challenged, but we also need to be encouraged and supported. Tough talking only goes so far. Tough love goes further.

Second Sunday before Lent

Creation and Anxiety

Genesis 1:1–23   Romans 8:18–25

Psalm 136   Matthew 6:25–end

In the beginning God created the heavens and the earth. The earth was a vast waste, darkness covered the deep, and the spirit of God hovered over the surface of the water. God said, 'Let there be light,' and there was light.

GENESIS 1:1

"*This is why I tell you not to be anxious about food and drink to keep you alive and clothes to cover your body. Surely life is more than food, the body more than clothes. Look at the birds in the sky; they do not sow and reap and store in barns, yet your heavenly Father feeds them. Are you now worth more than the birds? Can anxious thought add a single day to our life?*"

MATTHEW 6:25–27

"*Set your mind on God's kingdom and his justice before everything else, and all the rest will come to you as well. So do not be anxious about tomorrow; tomorrow will look after itself. Each day has troubles enough of its own.*"

MATTHEW 6:33–34

There is a magnificence and an endearing simplicity in the creation story in Genesis. However much I reject the story as merely engaging fantasy that flies in the face of science and reason, I have to acknowledge an admiration for the power of the storytelling. God acts with masterly simplicity. When he tells things to happen, they happen, and they are good. How could they not be? God would not be God if he had to think twice, or re-do something that was not quite as perfect as he would like.

We can read the creation story as a poetic yet practical explanation that satisfies our never-ending questioning about how the world began which evolutionary science can never quite erase from our minds. In fact the more we learn about the origins of the universe, the more we are baffled by impenetrable discussions of mass, energy, black holes, and the Big Bang, the more we yearn for a simple and satisfying explanation.

At another level, the Genesis story challenges us to think about the very nature of God. Michelangelo's fresco on the ceiling of the Sistine Chapel offers us a strong, older man, with flowing white hair and beard, good muscle tone, surrounded by well-fed cherubs, all floating in a void, yet wrapped in a cloak, as he puts the finishing touch, literally, to his creation, Adam. It is an appealing image that fills our need both for cosmic explanation and kindly parenting.

The Genesis story does not make it that easy. There is great mystery here: *The spirit of God hovered over the surface of the water.* Some translations talk about a wind blowing, but the Spirit of God "hovering" suggests to me something more ethereal, insubstantial and unworldly, that within itself has the power of creation. The more, both in knowledge and time, I try to understand this, the less I can. I am tempted by an explanation couched in human terms that makes no sense in the context of the very thing I am trying to explain. I am thrown back on my own devices asking, "What do I really believe about all this?"

In the verses from Matthew, Jesus says that we get nowhere by worrying. He offers us two contrasting ways of looking at the world, that echo our different responses to the creation story in Genesis.

On one level we can take confidence from God's creation, the birds in the sky, and (in later verses) the lilies in the field. God looks after them, so it is logical to assume that he will look after us. The words are very familiar to us, and they do indeed capture our imagination, even though the logic is questionable. We understand the process of evolution that has made birds, animals and plants the way they are now, and therefore we are less prepared to believe that their well-being depends on God's intervention, even if we would like to.

I am very attracted to the notion that there is no value or virtue in anxious thoughts. There is no point in worrying about food, drink, and clothes, not because "God will provide" as the image of the birds suggests, but because they are not the most important things in life. *Life is more than food, the body more than clothes.* Look no further than Maslow's hierarchy of needs for modern thinking that recognises the importance of, in his words, "self-actualisation" as the state to which we should aspire to make the fullest sense of our creation and our humanity.

Jesus and Matthew take this argument further in the following verses. If we concentrate on our understanding of *God's kingdom and his justice*. If we focus on the higher, more spiritual, aspects of life, and pay attention to how in our own way we may create a more just and fair world, everything else will begin to make sense. Part of me wants to believe that very much indeed.

Jesus recognises that this is not as straightforward as it sounds. Daily life, represented literally and metaphorically by food, drink, and clothes, gets in the way. I find myself spending time worrying about the more mundane aspects of existence, at the expense of less selfish and more spiritual things. Each day does indeed have *troubles enough of its own* but if we worry about them less, we will have time and space to pursue other aspects of life, that have greater meaning because through them we will come to understand why we are here.

Why we are here is a far more important question that how did we come to be here? For me, the mystery of creation is less about how it happened, and more about why it happened. The only way to discover that is to live the life we have been given. I can tie myself up in intellectual knots trying to understand the mysteries of creation and the enormity of the universe, but it does not get me anywhere. It does not add a single day to my life, and probably quite the opposite. Killing myself with worry about how the world began defeats its object.

SUNDAY NEXT BEFORE LENT

Clouds of Not Knowing

Exodus 24:12–end   2 Peter 1:16–end
Psalm 2   Matthew 17:1–9

Moses entered the cloud and went up the mountain; there he stayed forty days and forty nights.

EXODUS 24:18

Six days later Jesus took Peter, James, and John the brother of James, and led them up a high mountain by themselves. And in their presence he was transfigured; his face shone like the sun, and his clothes became brilliant white. And they saw Moses and Elijah appear, talking with him. Then Peter spoke: 'Lord,' he said, 'it is good that we are here. Would you like me to make three shelters here, one for you, one for Moses, and one for Elijah?'

MATTHEW 17:1–4

While he was still speaking, a bright cloud suddenly cast its shadow over them, and a voice called from the cloud: 'This is my beloved Son, in whom I take delight; listen to him.' At the sound of his voice the disciples fell on their knees in terror. Then Jesus came up to them, and said, 'Stand up, do not be afraid.' And when they raised their eyes there was no one but Jesus to be seen.

MATTHEW 17:5–8

Moses, we are told, went up a mountain, experienced a strong presence of God, and after extensive advice and instruction eventually came down again with the Ten Commandments inscribed by God on stone tablets.

Matthew describes the experience of Peter, James and John who accompanied Jesus up another mountain, saw him "transfigured", and heard the voice of God commending his Son to them.

It is difficult to know what to do with these stories. Do we dismiss them as fantasies that are irrelevant to our lives today? Do we accept them as literary (rather than literal) descriptions of the close connections between God and man, then and now? Or do we allow elements of the stories to seep into our consciousness and stimulate new trains of thought? My choice is the last of these, and I hold on to four elements: clouds, contentment, fear, and change. These four seem to me to have in them the essential characteristics of all really powerful experiences.

Clouds are one of the hallmarks of critical events in both the Old and the New Testament. It is not difficult to see why. We may be meteorologically more sophisticated, but the message of the clouds must be no different now than it was then. We enjoy the continuous movement and shape-changing of the clouds. We delight in vivid sunsets and dawn light. We are anxious about looming storm clouds, or a clouded sky that is heavy with rain or snow. We scuttle long with our heads bowed as the rain pours down. We know it is nothing personal, but it feels like it, so it is not surprising that we hark back to former beliefs and say, only partly in jest—"What have we done to deserve this weather?"

The writers of Exodus and Matthew captured the anxieties that sudden clouds bring, the sun is obscured, and shadows pass over us. What seemed clear and bright is suddenly less so. This is a vivid description of the perplexities that can suddenly overcome us all. A thought, or an experience, or an event elsewhere can suddenly throw some of our carefully held convictions into doubt. We can no longer see where we are going. We have to stop until the cloud clears from our minds, and we see things in a new light.

Moses, we are asked to believe, overcame his fear, stayed on the mountain for the proverbial forty days and forty nights, and enjoyed a close and exhausting lecture from God. The disciples saw an amazing transformation of Jesus and the appearance of two long-dead prophets. This was enough to terrify anyone, and send them running down the mountain to safety and to preserve their sanity. Nothing like that happened. Not only did Peter say that he felt it was good to be there, but he wanted them to protect themselves from the weather and stay there longer. The message here is that we need to respond to the feeling of the moment, because there are times when our heart, or our gut-feeling, may be more powerful than our mind.

The disciples' confidence and sense of well-being was then completely destroyed by the voice of God calling from the cloud. That really did terrify them. They had now become part of an experience that their minds simply could not cope with. They literally cowered, as we might in the face of any real or imaginary horror. Whatever they believed about Jesus until that moment was now completely changed. What on earth were they going to do now? Then Jesus, we assume quietly and kindly, tells them not to be afraid, and to their great relief the clouds cleared and he was standing there alone. They had had a revelatory experience that had changed their view of the world. They now saw Jesus' relationship to God and the past in an entirely new light, but could they handle it?

In our emotional vocabulary clouds are usually a bad thing. They suggest sadness, depression, obscurity, and storms. We know they are physically insubstantial, but they are all encompassing and it is impossible to see through them. Life's difficulties have all those characteristics. If we cannot see our way forward, and feel threatened or challenged, it is very difficult to find the mental strength to proceed. We may believe that it will all come right in the end. The problem is that things frequently do not, or at least not in the way we expect them to.

I can recognise that many people will take comfort from the experiences of Moses and the disciples and see their stories as a strengthening of faith into a new understanding of God. I am not comfortable with that. For me there are times when the clouds are simply all there is. I don't know what they are for. I don't know what they mean. I don't know whether I will get through them. I don't know what things will look like when they are gone. I do, however, believe that not knowing is the cloud we all live in.

Ash Wednesday

Ritual Reminders

Joel 2:1–2, 12–17   2 Corinthians 5:20b–6.10
Psalm 51:1–18   Matthew 6:1–6, 16–21

From my birth I have been evil, sinful from the time my mother conceived me. You desire faithfulness in the inmost being, so teach me wisdom in my heart.

PSALM 51:5–6

We recommend ourselves by innocent behaviour and grasp of truth, by patience and kindliness, by gifts of the Holy Spirit, by unaffected love, by declaring the truth, by the power of God. We wield the weapons of righteousness in right hand and left.

2 CORINTHIANS 6:6–7

'Be careful not to parade your religion before others; if you do, no reward awaits you with your Father in heaven.'

MATTHEW 6:1

Ash Wednesday. The start of Lent. Fasting. Acknowledging our failings. Penance. A cross in ashes on the forehead. Identifying with Christ. Recognising our mortality. In the medieval world of monks, hair shirts, self-flagellation, authoritarian priests, and a mortal fear of hell, all this makes some kind of historical but aberrant sense. That was then. This is now. Yet, even the most modern and irreligious will be heard to say, "What am I going to give up for Lent this year?"

In our nominally Christian lives we have entrenched in our minds the thought that giving something up at this time of year is a good thing to do. This will have nothing to do with any sense of moral failings. We will have no thought of the symbolism of Easter to come. It will just be a small, private gesture—no chocolate, less wine, more kindness—that makes sense to us.

Paul in his letter to the Corinthians concisely sets out the Christian case:

> *"Christ was innocent of sin, and yet for our sake God made him one with human sinfulness, so that in him we might be made one with the righteousness of God."*—2 Corinthians 5:21

I cannot count the number of times I have heard these words, and others very similar repeated from the pulpit, the lectern, and in prayers, but repetition does not aid understanding.

I find the concept of our essential, inherent sinfulness very difficult to take. I just do not believe it. The Psalmist makes it plain. In his words my sinfulness is not just from birth, but from conception. The whole of my life must therefore be devoted to finding a way to make amends for this through behaviour that is acceptable to God. I can fully accept that growing up involves a loss of innocence, keeping to any kind of moral high ground is difficult, and our failure to do so is often a cause for regret. That is how life is. On the other hand, for us to be burdened with a permanent guilt for some illusory failure in an imagined past is to me a betrayal of what humanity is. Guilt is not creative. Blame is demeaning. Penance is inward-looking and self-serving. So why does Lent have such a hold on us?

For me there is a value in any sincerely observed ritual that offers a steady reminder of some greater and more complex truth. This does not have to be anything grand or public. If it is important to me, and it makes me think, that is all that I need.

The verses above from the Second Letter to the Corinthians and Matthew's gospel give us some helpful pointers. Matthew records Jesus' advice that we should not make an ostentatious fuss about our religious observance. He says that we must pray in secret, give to charity in secret, and fast in secret because *"Your Father who sees what is done in secret will reward you."* Whatever we may or may not believe about God and Jesus, we can live with an understanding that somehow that is already known to God anyway. We do what we do because it makes sense to us. Because it makes sense to us it makes sense to God, even if we do not believe in him. But does that make sense?

Paul's Letter to the Corinthians explains how Christian ministers at that time, and now, should behave as a model for others to follow. If this is a definition of *righteousness*, which itself brings us closer to God, it is a good way to live, irrespective of any background noise about being evil since birth. Doing good things is very simply a good thing to do.

In the verses that follow those above Paul sets out the paradoxes that characterise the lives of Christian ministers:

> *Honour and dishonour, praise and blame, are alike our lot; we are the imposters who speak the truth, the unknown men whom all men know; dying we still live on; disciplined in suffering, we are not done to death; in our sorrows we have always cause for joy; poor ourselves, we bring wealth to many; penniless, we own the world.*
> —2 Corinthians 6:8–10

The last two thousand years in which many people have shown the power of the human spirit to rise above persecution, torture, imprisonment and death, is testament enough to the truth of these words.

We may not be blessed with such saintliness, nor faced with such extremes of abuse and suffering, but we will from time to time feel the need to rise above all the depressing things in human life that pull us down and further destroy any vestiges of goodness we hang on to. We will *own the world* by feeling better about ourselves and our place in it.

Giving up something for Lent is a small, ritual gesture that acknowledges this need and this desire. Not doing something is a simple prompt that we could do so much more.

First Sunday of Lent
Tempting Offers

Genesis 2:15–17; 3:1–7   Romans 5:12–19
Psalm 32   Matthew 4:1–11

'We may eat the fruit of any tree in the garden, except for the tree in the middle of the garden. God has forbidden us to eat the fruit of that tree or even touch it; if we do, we shall die.' 'Of course you will not die,' said the serpent; 'for God knows that, as soon as you eat it, your eyes will be opened and you will be like God himself, knowing both good and evil.'

GENESIS 3:2–5

The woman looked at the tree: the fruit would be good to eat; it was pleasing to the eye and desirable for the knowledge it could give. So she took some and ate it; she also gave some to her husband, and he ate it. Then the eyes of both of them were opened, and they knew that they were naked.

GENESIS 3:6–7

Jesus was then led by the Spirit into the wilderness, to be tempted by the devil. For forty days and nights he fasted, and at the end of them he was famished.

MATTHEW 4:1

TEMPTING OFFERS

The Lord's Prayer contains the words "Lead us not into temptation." We are so familiar with the words that their oddity and contradiction has been eroded by time and repetition. Modern translations of Christ's original words are more helpful: "Do not put us to the test." This suggests that the traditional line is less about asking God not to lead us to something that is contrary to his very nature, but a request that he helps us to avoid the things that will be morally destructive to our lives. The problem is that this interpretation of the request contradicts our understanding of the nature of life itself. The world would not be the world if there were no difficulties, challenges, choices, temptations that we have to deal with on a daily basis. If it was, metaphorically we would still be in the Garden of Eden.

The Genesis account of the creation of Adam and Eve, the Garden of Eden, the Tree of Knowledge, the wily serpent, gullible but far-sighted Eve, trusting Adam, self-discovery, fear, and expulsion is a great story. No wonder we hold on to it, so that even if we don't believe it, it becomes part of our belief system. The power of the story is that the characters are believable and their words convincing, so much so that we accept their validity. The serpent rejects God's restrictions and explains why, with an argument that misunderstands the nature of God. This sets up in us a challenge to wonder about the writers of Genesis accrediting God with a moral view that is itself entirely human.

Eve has always been given a very bad press. She may be guilty of taking the serpent's words at face value (and who wouldn't), but she recognises that the fruit is as appetising as the things she will know when she has eaten it. Where is the downside?

The story falls apart in that the first result of eating (as we usually say) the apple, is that Adam and Eve know that they are naked. This is not our understanding of a *knowledge of good and evil* , but it does set up attitudes to gender and sex that have bedevilled (appropriate choice of word in this context) society ever since.

My difficulty is that whilst I enjoy that story, I cannot accept it, or believe it, as the premise upon which the explanation and justification of Christ's life and death is based. This, for me, is the equivalent of using *Breaking Bad* as the rationale for not teaching chemistry in schools. Fact based on fiction does not work for me.

An alternative argument with which I have great sympathy is that nothing in the Bible is literal. It is all poetry, metaphor, and symbolism, the result of the attempts by many people over many years to make sense of their experiences, beliefs, and understanding of the deeper and more mysterious things of life. That being the case, metaphor based on metaphor is an imaginative way to stimulate thought.

Out of this fiction comes a view of the nature temptation. Christ faced his most vividly when he rejected the opportunity to demonstrate his powers by changing stones to bread, jumping off a high building, and accepting world domination. He had the mental strength and internal arguments to recognise that these temptations were of spurious value. They would not serve his wider purpose because people would respond to his powers not his person.

My own temptations have within them all the elements in these stories. A moral code or prohibition that forbids an action. A convincing argument that the premise upon which the prohibition is based is dubious, valueless, or serves another's interest rather than our own. A rationalisation of that argument in our own minds. An acceptance of its truth with the belief that our interest will be better served by doing rather than not doing. Sharing this conviction with someone else to bolster resolve and gain support. Action. External or internal recrimination. Rejection by those we have let down, or by society itself. A sense of personal failure. Far reaching negative consequences.

My ability to resist temptation is the ability to take the long view, to look beyond the immediate attractions to consequences further down the line, and to recognise that I 'have been here before' and all too often, have failed before. When I am struggling with temptations that are personal rather than public, I do not always learn from past mistakes. The very nature of temptation is that at some level it remains tempting.

I believe that our ability to deal with temptations of all sorts, large and small, makes us who we are. These internal struggles hone our behaviour, personality, and what we so aptly call 'strength of character'. In our lives we will face many situations when short term opportunities of dubious value seem eminently more attractive than longer term moral certainties. We will also discover many people whose lives and behaviour we can emulate, and some we can trust with our deepest moral quandaries. We need help from them to deal with temptation because it will not go away.

Second Sunday of Lent
Uncomfortable Words

Genesis 12:1–4a   Romans 4:1–5, 13–17
Psalm 121   John 3:1–17

If someone does a piece of work, his wages are not 'counted' to be a gift; they are paid as his due. But if someone without any work to his credit simply puts his faith in him who acquits the wrongdoer, then is faith is indeed 'counted as righteousness'.

ROMANS 4:4–5

'You ought not to be astonished when I say, "You must all be born again." The wind blows where it wills; you hear the sound of it, but you do not know where it comes from or where it is going. So it is with everyone who is born from the Spirit.'

JOHN 3:7–8

God so loved the world that he gave his only Son, that everyone who has faith in him may not perish, but have eternal life. It was not to judge the world that God sent his Son into the world, but that through him the world might be saved.

JOHN 3:16–17

THE IDEA OF BEING 'born again' makes me uncomfortable. People who claim to have been 'born again' are describing an experience that I cannot understand, and therefore cannot relate to. That in itself does not diminish or denigrate what they say has happened to them, it simply makes me question what it really means. Does it set them apart from me, or me apart from them? In the eyes of God, is there any difference between us? Are they in some mysterious way 'better' people than I am? Have they joined a club for the spiritually elite? If so, would I want to belong to it?

My own feeling is that it is just not that simple. The vocabulary of being 'born again' and of being 'saved' suggests a one-off event, or unique experience, during or after which eyes are opened, a new understanding is reached, and a special and very personal relationship with Jesus Christ is formed. For me, human life is far too complex and morally ambiguous for that to be an answer, or even the answer, to what the Christian faith is telling us.

The three passages above contain three fundamental concepts that I have heard expounded and interpreted from pulpit after pulpit. I am told that I need to live by faith, and from that will come my reward, in heaven. I am told that my life needs to be renewed via some form of spiritual rebirth. I am told that through my belief in Christ I will be saved from a sinful inheritance and enjoy eternal life. I could never understand any of this. I took it on trust. It appeared to be what everyone else was doing, but I was not sure whether it made one jot of difference to the way I lived, behaved, and what I thought was important in life. Where does that leave me now?

The repetition of mysterious concepts and their incorporation into statements of religious "truth" does not itself give them validity. We are lulled into a blind acceptance that ideas and statements that are first found in the Bible, and have been repeated and interpreted ever since as axiomatic to the Christian faith, must be "true" whether we understand them or not. That seems to me to be counter-intuitive.

I know that many will argue that this is the whole point of faith. We have to live through doubts uncertainties, and clouds of obscurity. We believe, in some way that goes beyond understanding, that there is a greater force at work in the world and in our lives. That force, or spirit, will ultimately bring us understanding though that may not be in this lifetime or in this world. Guided by all this we will be better, more Christ-like, people. That is what God, who created us, wants. That is what makes sense of his creation and our lives.

Whilst that seems an awful lot to ask, I wrote that paragraph without any inner cynicism. At some level I can understand and accept all that means something, even if I am not sure what. That for me is the essence of the problem.

We can all debate the real meaning of being born again, and of faith, and of salvation, and of eternal life, literally for ever. The words, explanations, and personal testimonies of one person or group will be a complete turn off for another. Positions become polarised and views entrenched. People and churches become divided by their opinions. The beliefs that are founded on what is best for humanity create exactly the opposite. Faith that goes beyond time, faith that stretches our imagination, faith that is a force for good, becomes temporal, petty, and divisive.

I need a freedom to wrestle with the uncertainties of belief, and my negative reaction to the concept of being born again grows out of a feeling that such certainty denies the importance of the struggle. I attend church services rarely because they seem to be demonstrating and preaching conviction to the convinced, and I am not. They are offering answers when I have only questions.

For me, the most telling sentence in the passages above is Jesus' analogy of spirit and wind. My conviction is that there is something beyond our human comprehension in our lives that for convenience we may call the spirit of God. Understanding what this means, how it works, and gauging our response to it is a continuous struggle. We sometimes have glimmers of understanding that throw a new light on ourselves and our lives. They are only glimmers but enough to build our confidence. Confidence that it is a good thing to be open to such mysterious influences, the sudden insights that blow into our minds, the unexpected lifting of mental fog, the awareness of new possibilities. Confidence that the accumulation of these experiences does give meaning and purpose to our lives. Confidence that in our personal experience we can begin, in some small and struggling way, to grapple with the ideas and concepts of faith, salvation, eternal life, and being born again, using words that make sense to each of us, in our own way.

Third Sunday of Lent
Meat and Drink

Exodus 17:1–7   Romans 5:1–11

Psalm 95   John 4:5–42

Christ died for us while we were yet sinners, and that is God's proof of his love towards us. And so, since we have now been justified by Christ's sacrificial death, we shall all the more certainly be saved through him from final retribution.

Romans 5:8–9

Jesus answered, "Everyone who drinks this water will be thirsty again, but whoever drinks the water I shall give will never again be thirsty. The water that I shall give will be a spring of water within him, welling up and bringing eternal life." " Sir," said the woman, "give me this water, and then I shall not be thirsty, nor have to come all this way to draw water."

John 4:13–15

"I have food to eat of which you know nothing." At this the disciples said one to another, "Can someone have brought him food?" But Jesus said, "For me it is meat and drink to do the will of him who sent me until I have finished his work."

John 4:32–34

MEAT AND DRINK

THERE IS NOT MUCH opportunity to laugh out loud at readings from the Bible. There is a great deal of "rejoicing" but separated by two thousand years this hardly raises a smile today. I wonder if the odour of sanctity has conditioned us into thinking that a more boisterous response would be inappropriate or disrespectful. If so, it is a pity.

It is clear that the impact of Christ's teaching and his life was immediate. People met him and followed him. People listened to what he had to say, and it changed their lives. People were touched by him, physically and mentally, and their pains and heartaches disappeared. One of their responses must have been to laugh out loud, with excitement, joy, and relief. We can only assume that he did too. It would have been inhuman not too. It would be sad if we lost this laughter in the sobriety of our response to what we are reading or hearing.

In these two passages from John we have rare exceptions to this rule. The writer, and his translators, show masterly comic timing to highlight the enormous gulf between Christ's words and prosaic, human responses to them.

The women takes the promise of water at face value, and revels in the thought that she will no longer have to walk a long distance to collect water from a well, and then trudge home with it. She is delighted at the thought. The disciples can only assume that Jesus is talking about a quick meal he has taken recently without any of them knowing about it. They are puzzled and a little jealous as up to now they have eaten together daily.

We laugh at the lack of understanding, and feel a little superior that we know better. Deep down, however, there is a nagging feeling that if we were the woman and the disciples, our reaction would be exactly the same. It gives us pause for thought to wonder whether in our own lives we have taken a superficial view of something profound and life-changing.

Paul, in his letter to the Romans, recalls the power of Christ's preaching, but he lacks the skill to present complex ideas in an easily digestible form. He gives us a form of words that has become the ecclesiastical norm: *Christ died for us while we were yet sinners. God's proof of his love towards us. Sacrificial death. Saved though him from final retribution.* Subsequent over-use and over-familiarity has created an acceptance that belies their obscurity. This is difficult stuff. For me, it begs many questions.

Am I still a "sinner" in the eyes of the church? Does the concept of a "sacrifice" have any meaning today? God has no human characteristics so how can we understand the nature of his love? What does being saved really mean? Is 'final retribution' simply the stuff of Old Master paintings, and medieval murals? What would we be punished for? Surely life only makes sense if we live it to the full. It makes no sense if we live it in fear of death and whatever comes afterwards.

By contrast, Christ's simple words and images—*water, thirst, meat, drink*—capture my imagination in an entirely different way. He is offering something mysterious, yet mentally tangible. He is suggesting that this, whatever it is, will be deeply satisfying. He asks us to believe that our understanding of his meaning will last longer than we can ever imagine. It will have a far more profound effect on our lives than a glass of water or a meat stew.

The fact that the meaning of Christ's words is elusive makes me more determined to understand them. The writer of John's gospel was drawing on the memories and anecdotes of many who were with Jesus. The power of Christ's words had resisted the erosion of time and memory, so that even partial recollection demanded attention. That power remains.

I am forced to say to myself that there is more here than meets the eye, so I have to think deeper. I have to explore how, where, and why, the messages of Christ's life might make a difference to mine. My uncertainty about Paul's words remains, as does my distrust of pulpit platitudes and prayer-speech. I am deeply attracted by the immediacy of Christ's words, and of the stories that accompany them. The reaction of the woman and the disciples serves as simple counterpoint that highlights the profundity of what Christ is saying.

John captures all this with a masterly touch of theatre:

> '*God is spirit, and those who worship him must worship in spirit and in truth.*' *The woman answered,* '*I know that Messiah*' *(that is Christ)* '*is coming. When he comes he will make everything clear to us.*' *Jesus said to her,* '*I am he. I who am speaking to you.*'—John 4:24–26

For that reason I need to understand what Christ meant by '*The water I shall give will be a spring of water within him, welling up and bringing eternal life.*' Is this a belief system, a moral code, a philosophical concept, a form of behaviour, an ambition, a pious hope, or something that embraces yet goes beyond all those to be something that makes sense of all life, and my life. If that is so, meat and drink it is.

Annunciation of our Lord to the Blessed Virgin Mary

Questioning Acceptance

Isaiah 7:10–14
Psalm 40:5–11
Hebrews 10:4–10
Luke 1:26–38

Then the angel said to her, 'Do not be afraid Mary, for God has been gracious to you; you will conceive and give birth to a son, and you are to give him the name Jesus. He will be great, and will be called the Son of the Most High.'

Luke 1:30–32

'How can this be?' said Mary, 'I am still a virgin.' The angel answered, 'The Holy Spirit will come upon you, and the power of the Most High will overshadow you; for that reason the holy child to be born will be called Son of God.'

Luke 1:34–35

'I am the Lord's servant,' said Mary; 'may it be as you have said.' Then the angel left her.

Luke 1:38

IN MY PROTESTANT UPBRINGING I did not spend much time thinking about Mary the Mother of Jesus. I was aware that Roman Catholics took a rather different view, but for me Mary was out of sight and out of mind. It therefore came as quite a surprise in later to life to discover, on reading my father's books, and later tributes to him after his death, that he had a deep and profound devotion to Mary. For a Methodist, this was remarkable. For my father, with hindsight, less so. He had an ecumenical viewpoint, and among other books, had written a highly regarded book on the Rosary. For him, Mary was important, and I regret the fact that he is no longer here (he died in 1992) for me to ask him why.

For those of us who are not brought up and imbued with Marian devotion, she is a haunting and haunted figure. Her unique status as the mother of Jesus is confused by two things: there are a number of other Marys in the Gospels, some of whom may or may not be the mother of Jesus; and for someone who is regarded with such reverence, she appears very little.

In the Gospels we have only have seven glimpses of her life: pregnancy and threat of divorce; meeting with Elizabeth and praying the Magnificat; the birth of Jesus; visits of the shepherds and Wise Men; Jesus teaching in the synagogue; the marriage at Cana and turning the water into wine; and at the foot of the Cross. Some argue that Jesus also appeared to her after the Resurrection, but this is not clear from the Gospels. We know nothing about the influence she, and Joseph, had on Jesus as he was growing up. Once an adult his life overshadows hers until the moment of his death. Her story is therefore more tragic than glorious, characterised by troubles and perplexities that we are told she keeps to herself, suffering in silence.

The mechanics of Jesus' conception are as mysterious to us as they were to her, and will ever remain so. It serves no purpose to explore divine gynaecology and obstetrics, or to argue that there was nothing divine about it. Even if the conception and birth were not extraordinary, the child certainly was, and our understanding of human nature tells us that Mary must have had a major influence on what he became. That deserves our respect and devotion.

For me, Mary represents the best and the most trusting in us all, giving us a difficult model to follow. Faced with a unique and outstanding opportunity that we do not really understand, is our natural instinct to accept without question or to challenge and interrogate for more details? Mary's immediate reaction was the latter, *"How can this be?"* The answer she was given went

QUESTIONING ACCEPTANCE

beyond her wildest expectations, makings matters worse not better, and yet she accepted what was going to happen. Would we do the same?

We live in a world of logical analysis, scientific explanations, and causal connections. Our world distrusts magic and the unexplained. We are encouraged to think strategically, beyond the present moment to what might happen, or could happen, or should happen. We adopt defensive positions, encouraged to hope for the best, yet prepare for the worst. We have little trust that outcomes will be good. We believe, for most of the time, that if something can go wrong it will. This is a very sad state of affairs.

I know that there are people whose faith and 'trust in God' is such that they can with all honesty echo Mary's words: *'I am the Lord's servant, may it be as you have said.'* I am not one of them. Sometimes I wish I was. Yet I can imagine a scenario in which initial hope and trust is eroded or challenged by setbacks so severe that it seems impossible to proceed. Fortunately history is full of people whose mettle has been proved by such situations. They have gone on to reach even greater heights of success than they first imagined. I doubt whether I am one of those.

Most of us operate at a more modest level. The challenges we face will not change the world, except in a very small way. The risks we run are easy to mitigate. Our judgment is sound. We can articulate the pros and cons of any opportunity. Our mind usually rules our heart. This is me, but is it the only way to live? How can I go beyond the constraints of my personality and mental processes to accept something personal and profound that goes beyond everything I understand?

We all, I think, aspire to great things, and would like to make a small difference to the world. I share that view but I am troubled by its arrogance. At the same time I know that I have only a very vague understanding of my impact on others. The 'sweetness and light' that I believe I exude is seen very differently by others. My positives become their negatives. If my judgement of myself and my impact on others is so faulty, how will I ever know when and how my behaviour will make a positive difference?

If my aspirations are modest, and my self-esteem moderate, how will I respond to any message, whether spiritual, emotional, or cerebral, that suggests that I must do something extraordinary? Is my automatic response questioning and accepting, or simply rejecting because it is beyond my understanding of myself and the world?

Fourth Sunday of Lent
Seeing and Believing

I Samuel 16:1–13   Ephesians 5:8–14

Psalm 23   John 9:1–39

'The Lord does not see as a mortal sees; mortals see only appearances but the Lord sees into the heart.'

1 Samuel 16:7

So for the second time they summoned the man who had been blind, and said, "Speak the truth before God. We know that this man is a sinner." " Whether or not he is a sinner, I do not know," the man replied. "All I know is this: I was blind and now I can see."

John 9:24–25

"How extraordinary! Here is a man who has opened my eyes, yet you do not know where he comes from! We know that God does not listen to sinners; he listens to anyone who is devout and obeys his will. To open the eyes of a man born blind—that is unheard of since time began. If this man was not from God he could do nothing."

John 9:30–32

SEEING AND BELIEVING

A COMPLEX INTERLOCKING PATTERN of themes of sight and blindness, both actual and spiritual run through the verses above.

In the verse from Samuel seeing what is in front of our eyes, the presenting facts, is contrasted with the ability to look deeper. This is cited as the difference between God and man, but for me it is the difference between the worldly and the spiritual. To understand the world and my place in it, to find the deeper meaning of why I am here, I need to look below the surface into my motivations, passions, hopes, and fears. At the same time as learning to know myself (as Socrates advocated) I have to learn to "see into the heart" of everyone I have dealings with. If the true worth and value of everyone lies beneath the surface then we owe it to each other to find a way of getting in touch with that inner essence, or soul, as that is where their true nature lies.

In John's account of the healing of the blind man, the Jewish authorities see what has happened but are blinded by prejudice and their moral code and fail to understand its true meaning. The man who was blind and can now see challenges their view of the world with logic and hard facts, and then expresses amazement at their inability to recognise who has just healed him. The authorities had already judged Jesus' behaviour. In their eyes, he had broken their laws and codes of conduct and was therefore beyond the pale. In their eyes, a man like Jesus could not perform miraculous acts of healing so there must be some other reason for the man regaining his sight. He on the other hand punctures their posturing with a simple statement of fact, throwing it back to them to find the reason. Then realising this is getting nowhere, he spells it out, and the authorities *"turn him out"* of the place to which they had summoned him, presumably with a mixture of anger, pique and frustration.

My own inability to understand "where someone is coming from" frequently sets up wilful blindness to their better qualities, and causes me to question their actions and distrust their motives. We all label people, with very little hard evidence to support such judgements. With a mixture of prejudice, presumption and wilful ignorance we say that someone is arrogant, ambitious, bigoted or any number of other pejorative words, and from that entrenched judgement comes our view of what they have done and what we expect them to do. Even more insidious is the fact that we suspect the motivation behind even the most caring and charitable action. We see what we have conditioned ourselves to expect, something negative and undesirable, and we are blind to any possibility that the opposite might be the case.

This begs a fundamental question about our view of humanity as a whole. Are people essentially "good" or essentially "evil"? Does thinking the best of people inevitably lead to disappointment and pain? Is thinking the worst of people the only sensible defense mechanism?

The answer is not straightforward. If it was, we would not need to ask the question. I can think of any number of people who "I don't really like" because "they are not my kind of person" or because of some real or imagined slight or rejection, often going back years, that does not really stand up to scrutiny now. Fortunately I can think of more people that I do like. With them I feel a close affinity of attitudes, values and behaviour, and most important of all I have a sense that they like me. In both cases I see what I want to see. On rare occasions I have been surprised by a change of heart on both sides, but this has never happened often enough to challenge my instincts about other people.

Does all this mean that I am spiritually blind, or at least short-sighted, so that I do not see the positives in one group and the negatives in another? Do I give people the benefit of the doubt and believe that they are not as "bad" as they seem? Do I blight my attitudes to my friends by thinking the worst of them? The truth is, of course, sometimes, but rarely. On the other hand, I would be the first to admit the opposite form of blindness: seeing only the worst in the people I do not like, and only the best in the people that I do.

I am on a hiding to nowhere to think like this. Doubting my own judgement, adopting entrenched attitudes, and questioning others' motives is guaranteed to lead to sorrow, anger, disappointment, and probably a lonely old age. Along with the man who was blind we have to say to ourselves, and others, "For goodness sake, something really good has happened here. Don't question it. Accept it at face value for the good that it is. Think more deeply about where that good has come from. Learn from this." We have to see and believe.

For the world to be a good place to live in, and for our lives to be fulfilling, rewarding and of value to other people, I believe that we have to say with Julian of Norwich "All shall be well, and all shall be well, and all manner of thing shall be well."

Fifth Sunday of Lent

Sorrowful Doubts

Ezekiel 37:1–14   Romans 8:6–11
Psalm 130   John 11:1–45

Jesus said, "I am the resurrection and the life. Whoever has faith in me shall live, even though he dies; and no one who lives and has faith in me shall ever die. Do you believe this?"

John 11:25–26

When Jesus saw her weeping and the Jews who had come with her weeping, he was moved with indignation and deeply distressed. "Where have you laid him?" he asked. They replied, "Come and see." Jesus wept.

John 11:33–35

The Jews said, "See how much he loved him!" But some of them said, "Could not this man, who opened the blind man's eyes, have done something to keep Lazarus from dying?"

John 11:36–37

The story of Lazarus was the start of this book. The Introduction explains how I was suddenly and unexpectedly struck with the full, dramatic impact of the words "Jesus wept." These set me on a search for other places where the force of a verse or verses from the Bible made me sit up, open my eyes, and think afresh about what they meant to me. The story of Lazarus has a much greater importance than those two words.

This Sunday is the beginning of Passiontide. Our thoughts move forward only a matter of days to Good Friday and Easter. In the Gospel stories Jesus knows that he is moving closer and closer to the end of his life. He has little time left to get his message across. He must have been torn apart by conflicting emotions, fear of what was to come, frustration that he had so much to do and so little time in which to do it, perplexity about how his followers would react to his death, uncertainty about what would come after that. No matter what was the actual chronology of events, it is fitting that this story comes at this time.

We cannot tell whether Jesus had any understanding or expectation of his own resurrection, but he did have a profound belief that faith in him and therefore in God would lead to some kind of life that goes on after death. I cannot imagine what "life after death" really means. I once had an abiding conviction that heaven was a warm and sunny place, where the ground was covered in parsley, the ideal combination of something edible and springy, great to lie on, because there would be little else to do.

It did not take me long to realise that any description of heaven in words that we use to talk about our life here was untenable. We have no way of understanding what "life after death" will be, so there is no way in which we can talk about it. That being the case, how on earth can we believe in it at all?

The Lazarus story carries within it all these doubts and anxieties, even in Jesus himself. For him there is the heart-searching question, could he have done anything to prevent Lazarus from dying?

Martha, Lazarus' sister, states quite openly that if Jesus had been there, close at hand, her brother would not have died. In the light of the healing that Jesus had already performed, this was a reasonable assumption. Jesus answers her practical challenge with a spiritual one to her. He asks her whether she believes that he is *'the resurrection and the life'*. Whether or not she understands what he means, she simply says that she believes he is the Son of God. For her that is enough, she does not need to explore the metaphysics of eternal life. We are left with the question, is that enough for us?

SORROWFUL DOUBTS

Then Jesus meets Martha's sister, Mary, who challenges him in exactly the same way, *"Lord, if you had been here, my brother would not have died."* She is weeping, her sister is weeping, everyone in the house is weeping, and Jesus is *"moved with indignation and deeply distressed."* This is more than sadness that a friend and follower has died. No wonder Jesus wept. For me, it suggests that Jesus silently agrees with Martha and Mary. He wonders whether he could have done more. He weeps with loss, he weeps with shared pain, he weeps with frustration, and he weeps with doubt. Does his inability to save Lazarus call in question both his powers and his mission? Was this the wrong thing or the right thing to do at the time? Would saving Lazarus have convinced more people of his purpose, or hastened his end?

Then he goes to the cave which was Lazarus' tomb, and makes his decision. *"Father, I thank you for hearing me. I know that you always hear me, but I have spoken for the sake of the people standing round, that they may believe it was you who sent me."* Then he calls Lazarus out of the tomb. This inspires many to *"put their faith in him"* but it also makes the chief priests and the Pharisees even more determined to get rid of him. His act of resurrection would hasten his own death.

It is easy to identify with the moments of human doubt and forthright challenge in this story. It is extremely difficult to understand the deeper meaning and expression of faith that Jesus requires of Mary. Yet put together the one informs and enlightens the other. That for me is why this story is so powerful. It demands attention.

The story of Lazarus starts with death and grief, embraces resentment and anger, hopes and disappointments, doubts and frustrations, and then ends with a living miracle, that is the start of a process that will lead to another death and another resurrection.

It does in itself not confirm belief. It does not in itself strengthen faith. It asks me to think about what I believe, and when I get to the limits of the believable, it asks me continue to believe, to have faith, in things that I cannot understand. It asks me to have faith in my doubts.

Palm Sunday
Triumph and Tragedy

Isaiah 50:4–9a Philippians 2:5–11
Psalm 118:19–24 Matthew 21:1–11

The stone which the builders rejected has become the main corner-stone.

Psalm 118:22

Take to heart among yourselves what you find in Christ Jesus: He was in the form of God; yet he laid no claim to equality with God, but made himself nothing, assuming the form of a slave. Bearing the human likeness, sharing the human lot, he humbled himself, and was obedient, even to the point of death, death on a cross.

Philippians 2:5–8

The disciples went and did as Jesus had directed, and brought the donkey and her foal; they laid their cloaks on them and Jesus mounted. Crowds of people carpeted the road with their cloaks, and some cut branches from the trees to spread on his path.

Matthew 21:6–8

TRIUMPH AND TRAGEDY

THERE IS GREAT TENSION between the excitement and expectation of the crowds that Jesus' entry into Jerusalem would herald major political and social change, and his own modest behaviour and awareness of his impending death. Did the crowds really believe that a prophesy in Zechariah 9: 9 was coming true: *'See, your king is coming to you, his cause won, his victory gained, humble and mounted on a donkey, on a colt, the foal of a donkey.'*? Or was this the wishful thinking of the Gospel writers? This is a tragedy, not a triumph. The people saw Jesus as something he was not. The trappings of a triumphal entry were inappropriate. The subsequent events were the opposite of anything that the crowds expected, but would ultimately have a greater impact than they ever dreamed.

Our expectations are so often conditioned by what we want to happen, and we interpret events accordingly, and then we are surprised and disappointed that things turn out differently. Is the problem one of ignorance or misguided hope? Do we need to learn to be wise before the event? Do we need to think deeper about the implications of what is happening, and always be at least five moves ahead? Would that we could. We often say "It seemed the right thing to do at the time" but only when we realise, from the pattern of subsequent events, that it was absolutely the wrong thing. The builders rejected the stone. Little did they know what it would become.

Our problem is always not knowing. We cannot see into the future. We cannot be certain of the impact of our actions on others. We cannot imagine how we will feel in the next hour, let alone the next day or year. All we can do is judge things as well as we can, with the limited knowledge and understanding at our disposal. So what was Christ thinking as he rode into Jerusalem on his donkey?

Christ's problem was that *'bearing human likeness, sharing the human lot, he humbled himself, and was obedient even to the point of death'*, yet he believed that the purpose of his life went far beyond the fact of his death.

Christ was certainly human, and suffered all the doubts and uncertainties that we do. Yet he clearly had some form of spiritual insight, some may call it divine, that enabled him to take a different view of the world from most people around him. Whilst there is no evidence that he could literally "see into the future", he had a view of life that went far beyond our limited understanding of birth and death. He preached this with force and passion, mixing difficult philosophical and metaphysical concepts with simple stories pregnant with meaning. He performed acts of healing that defied belief, yet persuaded people to believe in him. He offered personal encouragement to those on the margins of society that ran counter to the cultural norms of the time, yet persuaded people to behave differently.

I find that with so much of my reading of the Bible passages set for each Sunday the meaning that means most to me lies in contrasts and tensions: between Christ and other people, between the human and the divine, between the secular and the sacred, between conventional behaviour and new views of human life, between a reappraisal of triumph and a new understanding of tragedy.

The more I think about Christ in his moments of greatest stress, stress that is quintessentially human, when the tensions are the greatest, the more I come to realise and acknowledge that I need to think more deeply about what his life means. This is completely unexpected. When I started writing this book I was prepared to follow wherever my reading of the Bible passages and my reaction to them would lead me. I had no thought or plan when I reached Palm Sunday I would be writing as I have just done.

I was brought up from my earliest days on Bible stories that inevitably carried with them more sentiment than sense. As I grew older some of the deeper meaning became clearer, but the sentimentality never really went away. I understood that the entry into Jerusalem was anti-triumphal, emphasising humility not victory. Yet the excitement lay in the cheers and waving palms. That was where I was, celebrating something, I'm not sure what, triumphal. The pain and suffering to come was in the background, but kept at arm's length, yet for me now the only way any of the Palm Sunday story makes sense is to see Christ struggling with thoughts about what he has to face.

How would I behave in that situation? I have made an enormous and brave decision to do something I feel I cannot avoid. I feel humble and humbled by it, yet everyone else is shouting encouragement, praising me to the skies. *When he entered Jerusalem the whole city went wild with excitement. "Who is this?' people asked, and the crowds replied, 'This is the prophet Jesus, from Nazareth in Galilee.'* Heady stuff, tinged with parochial disbelief that a local boy from there had 'done good' to be here, like this. Would I be able to keep my feet on the ground? Would I shake my head in a deprecating, English way, "You're really making too much fuss." Or would I weep that they did not seem to understand? The truth is, I am one of them, and I still do not really understand.

Maundy Thursday

Significant Acts

Exodus 12:1–14   1 Corinthians 11:23–26
Psalm 116:1, 10–end   John 13:1– 7, 31b–35

On the night of his arrest the Lord Jesus took bread, and after giving thanks to God broke it and said: 'This is my body, which is for you; do this in memory of me.' In the same way, he took the cup after supper, and said: 'This cup is the new covenant sealed by my blood. Whenever you drink it, do this in memory of me.' For every time you eat this bread and drink the cup, you proclaim the death of the Lord, until he comes.

I Corinthians 11:23–26

You call me Teacher and Lord, and rightly so, for that is what I am. Then if I, your Lord and Teacher, have washed your feet, you also ought to wash one another's feet. I have set you an example: you are to do as I have done for you.

John 13:13–15

I give you a new commandment: love one another; as I have loved you, so you are to love one another. If there is love among you, then everyone will know that you are my disciples.

John 13:34–35

I HAVE USED THE words "Maundy Thursday" throughout my life, and have watched news bulletins of the Queen giving out "Maundy Money", but I had no idea what "Maundy" meant. Though it is perhaps more likely that I had been told once but had forgotten. The derivations are mixed. One group of scholars argues that it comes from the Latin for commandment and refers to the "new commandment" in John 13. Others claim it comes from the Latin, French, and English words meaning to beg, and refers to the alms given after services on this day. Whatever the origins, there are clear connections between these two meanings: loving others, whoever they are, and demonstrating that love through some form of giving.

Maundy Thursday is a day packed with biblical significance: Christ washing the disciples' feet, the Last Supper, betrayal by Judas, and Christ's arrest in the Garden of Gethsemane. So many of the events, stories, and teaching that are fundamental to Christian belief are represented here that Maundy Thursday deserves greater attention.

The day, as described in the Bible passages associated with it, is characterised by a number of very simple events that have far reaching and troubling significance. I find it difficult to work out what my personal response to examples of humble service, unconditional love, loyalty and betrayal, and liturgical rituals should be.

What and where in my life have been or should be the moments of humble service epitomised by the washing of the disciples' feet? Is this literally about finding ways to help the smelly and the dirty? Is it more subtle, an injunction to find ways to make other people feel better, spiritually and physically, by actions that show I really care? I am very uncomfortable with the former, but have some understanding of the value of the latter, though I rarely act on it.

Much has been written, preached, and argued about the nature of love. As we grow older we all learn that it is tougher than it sounds, carries with it happiness and heartache in equal measure, makes the world go round, can stop you in your tracks, change your life, and remain a mystery. The challenge we all face is how to love the unlovable, how to love those we don't like, how to love unconditionally. The *"new commandment"* is so simple in expression, but so difficult in delivery. The fact that Jesus referred to it as "new" is both a revelation and a revolution, and remains so.

Judas is always the villain of the piece. He appears briefly. Acts speedily. Dies unpleasantly. We tend to feel that he gets what he deserved, even when the accounts of his death in the New Testament differ. It is Judas' life before the Last Supper that interests me. I must assume that at some point Jesus chose him as a disciple. It makes no sense to me that he was chosen in the expectation that he would be a traitor to the cause. Jesus saw something in him that was commendable and fitted in with the team of disciples he was assembling. Judas, like us all, had conflicting agendas. Was he pleased to be chosen, yet dissatisfied with Jesus' message? Was he frustrated by spiritual teaching? Did he want action? Was he simply weak-willed, and open to bribes? Loyalty to a man like Jesus and his cause was not easy. I know that there is something of Judas in me, and in us all, His significance is much greater than his brief appearance might suggest.

The last problem is the Last Supper, a simple meal, at a critical time, with far-reaching significance. I have taken Holy Communion, celebrated the Eucharist, many times, and I am struck by how strange those words seem out of context. I know that at a superficial level I am not sure what I am doing or why I am doing it, yet at the time I have some sense of its symbolic and spiritual importance. My main stumbling blocks are the words. Two thousand years of repetition and sanctity have not made "This is my body" and "This is my blood" any easy to take, absorb, or digest. It is interesting that those words reflect the process of the ritual. What am I remembering and why?

From the pulpit I am reminded of Christ's life and teaching, of his death and resurrection, of Christian thinking about salvation and eternal life. I am encouraged to think deeply about the events of Christ's last days as leading me into a greater understanding of all that. The Eucharist becomes both a physical retelling and re-enactment of events that contained within them profound truths. In the moment, though, when I take the bread and sip the wine, where am I? I am kneeling, uncomfortable, puzzled, and slightly embarrassed.

I am also told that taking part in this ritual does not need to feel significant, every time, or any time. Being physically and emotionally part of the central and pivotal ritual of the Christian church is enough. Enlightenment and understanding will come. Paul's words to the Corinthians then take on a new significance. I have to be ready for the meaning of *"until he comes"* and hope that the Judas in me will not let me down.

Good Friday

Truth and Betrayal

Isaiah 52:13–53:end   Hebrews 10:16–25
Psalm 22   John 18:1–19:end

He was maltreated, yet he was submissive and did not open his mouth; like a sheep led to the slaughter, like a ewe that is dumb before the shearers, he did not open his mouth.

Isaiah 53:7

My God, my God, why have you forsaken me? Why are you so far from saving me, so far from heeding my groans? My God, by day I cry to you, but there is no answer; in the night I cry with no respite.

Psalm 22:1–2

'My task is to bear witness to the truth. For this I was born; for this I came into the world, and all who are not deaf to truth listen to my voice.' Pilate said, 'What is truth?' With those words he went out again to the Jews and said, 'For my part, I find no case against him.'

John 18:37–38

TRUTH AND BETRAYAL

WE LIVE IN A society that prides itself on its cultural sophistication and justice. We have rejected capital punishment, and find the thought of crowds attending beheadings or hangings as abhorrent as the punishment itself. We are appalled by street violence, murder, torture, or physical abuse of any kind. Yet we watch all those things for entertainment, and have become inured to their impact. The Crucifixion is so familiar to us in detail, but so far removed in time but we are unable to see it for what it was, drawn out capital punishment inflicting extreme suffering and humiliation.

Mel Gibson's 2004 film *The Passion of the Christ* was criticised for emphasising the violence and suffering, at the expense some thought of the deeper message. For me, to sanitise the pain and abuse, to coat suffering with sentiment, and to argue that the message is more important than the means by which it was conveyed is an aberration which makes nonsense of our Christian values and our humanity. Mel Gibson was right to show the blood, from the whipping, from the crown of thorns, from the carrying of the cross, from the nails. He was right to force us to listen to the jeers of the military, the abuse of the crowds, and Christ's final grunts and gasps of thirst and exhaustion as it became harder and harder to breath. I should be horrified, but familiarity means that I rarely am. I need to be reminded.

On the other hand, are the Gospel writers themselves subordinating the facts to get the message across? Harking back to the Old Testament there is talk of silent submission, sacrificial lambs, scapegoats, and dying "for our sins." The words of Christ on the cross and playing dice for his seamless garment are found in Psalm 22, and not breaking his legs in Psalm 34. Is this then an elaborate piece of fiction to make sense of events and give them a timeless significance, and thus sanitise a disgusting death?

The intensity of the humiliation, and the extremity of the pain throw into high relief other features of the Crucifixion that would have less impact in a less extreme context. In Luke's Gospel Christ forgives his abusers, in Matthew he cries out in the words of Psalm 22, and in John is suffering extreme thirst. For me these are other examples of the tension between Jesus' humanity and his relationship with God that make both more convincing. Whether or not the words *"My God, my God, why have you forsaken me"* are at heart a literary device, they ring true. It is because he is who he that he feels as he does. As his life ebbed did he compare his powerlessness with his former power? Did he ask what on earth is going on?

Pilate's words *"What is truth?"* only appear in John's Gospel. For me it does Pilate a great disservice to suggest that this was some kind of wry joke. Pilate was on the horns of a political dilemma which he was unable to resolve except by going against his own conscience. He was struggling with a decision that would be wrong in the eyes of one political group or other whatever he did. What was the right thing to do? May be he did see in Christ something that others did not see, but he still sent him to his death.

Pilate's question goes to the heart of everything that churches commemorate on Good Friday, and to our understanding of pain and suffering. We always ask why? Why me? Why this? Why that? Why now? Why them? We want to get to the truth, but we rarely do. We are left with more pain, and more uncertainty, as Christ was.

I have to ask myself whether I really understand the true meaning of Good Friday. I know that the Christian understanding of the importance of Easter lies in what comes afterwards. Resurrection needs death. Do I need to spend time thinking about an exhausted and bloody man hanging on a cross to make sense of all this? If I mentally follow Christ every step of the way, using Mel Gibson as my guide, am I any the wiser? To try to 'share the suffering' in some mysterious way, is simply to set up an antipathy to the horror, not an understanding of the meaning and purpose of the pain. It makes me want to run away, and I am not alone.

The sub-plot of the Good Friday story is Peter's experience. Jesus had seen through Judas and at the Last Supper had sent him on his way to do what he had to do. Almost in the same breath he tells Peter that he will deny that he knows him. Peter does just that. Three times. This is the second betrayal in a small and close-knit group of twelve people within a matter of hours. Peter must have been mortified at the truth of Christ's words, but at the time he had difficulty in believing them. I have to ask myself how often I have I rejected the truth of some less than endearing feature in my own character, only to face the harsh fact of its existence, and feel the resulting pain.

For me the lasting meaning of Good Friday is understanding where the truth of imagination meets the truth of experience, how we must work hard not to betray the things we value most when life becomes difficult, and if we do, how we endure the resulting pain.

EASTER DAY

Loss and Discovery

Exodus 14:10–end Acts 10:34–43
Psalm 118:14–24 John 20:1–18

We can bear witness to all that he did in the Jewish countryside and in Jerusalem. They put him to death, hanging him on a gibbet; but God raised him to life on the third day; and allowed him to be clearly seen, not by all people, but by witnesses whom God had chosen in advance— by us, who ate and drank with him after he rose from the dead.

ACTS: 10:39–41

She turned round and saw Jesus standing there, but she did not recognise him. Jesus asked her, 'Why are you weeping? Who are you looking for?' Thinking it was the gardener, she said. 'If it is you, sir, who have removed him, tell me where you have laid him and I shall take him away.' Jesus said 'Mary!' She turned and said to him 'Rabbuni!' (which is Hebrew for 'Teacher').

JOHN 20:14–16

'Do not cling to me,' said Jesus, 'for I have not yet ascended to the Father. But go to my brothers, and tell them that I am ascending to my Father and your Father, to my God and your God.' Mary of Magdala went to tell the disciples. 'I have seen the Lord,' she said, and gave them his message.

JOHN 20:17–18

After the bleak and harsh realities of Good Friday, we enter a new world on Easter Day. Churches are decorated, candles are lit, vestments change colour, and there is supposed to be an air of celebration, but it never quite feels like that. Although Easter should be spiritually more significant and profound than Christmas, it is far more difficult to comprehend. The default position is therefore to celebrate a human birth with much greater excitement and enthusiasm than a mysterious appearances after death. The facts of Christ "rising from the dead" are very difficult to handle. Accepting this is as a miracle beyond our comprehension, and "explaining" it in abstract terms does not work for me, but it demands serious thought.

As with Christmas, how it all happened matters little, because we can never know. It is pointless to try to explain the mystery of the empty tomb. I believe I need to move on from querying the facts then to explore the meaning. There are three things that capture my imagination and matter to me now: the appearances to only a few people; Mary's recognition; and Christ avoiding physical contact. For me these are fundamental to understanding what happened in human terms, which gives particular point to the deeper spiritual significance.

Only a small number of people had enjoyed a close relationship with Jesus. He had specifically chosen twelve disciples, and to them can be added his own and their own family members, and a few close friends. These were the people who were most closely involved in his death and burial, and who were most grief-stricken. Although Jesus had tried to explain to them, in his own way, what was going to happen, it is clear from their reaction that none of them had really believed him, or at least hoped that it would not be true. His death was therefore an appalling shock. Their sense of loss was as acute as their memory of his life. He was still with them in spirit, and his appearances "after death" are in my mind a description of this very natural phenomenon. Those who had felt closest to him felt he was still there.

Mary, in the garden, was blinded by her tears and angry that someone had, as she thought, stolen the body. She was in no state of mind to think of Jesus as being present because she was convinced of the opposite. Then something triggered a realisation that in her mind and heart he was there, and she had no need to look for him anymore.

Jesus tells her not to touch him, or in a more evocative translation "Do not cling to me." This is a masterly piece of storytelling as it uses our words to describe something that is on the edges of our comprehension. Jesus is telling her not to try to turn this experience into something physical. No matter how vivid Mary's imagination may be, he is not real in any physical sense. She should not cling to her memory of him as he was. She must look forward to a new understanding of him now that he is dead. Excited and encouraged by this new understanding, Mary rushes off using the only words she can *"I have seen the Lord."*

Easter makes sense now, for me, if I relate these three descriptions to my own understanding of the world. Not everybody has the wish or the ability to form a close relationship with God or to feel his presence with them at all times. I admire those who do, but I am skeptical because I struggle to understand what such a relationship would really feel like. I believe that we all approach spiritual issues in different ways, some more successfully than others. It is they who can offer guidance and help from their own experience. They may believe they have a calling to do this, or are surprised that they can. We need them.

It is very easy to be blind to the deeper things in life if I become obsessed with the frustrations pains and losses of the present moment. We often say that "We can't see for looking" which sums up our situation, and Mary's, exactly. The more I struggle to find something, the greater my frustration, the greater my anger, the greater the sense of loss, the greater the risk of not finding. So often what I am looking for turns up unexpectedly, with minimum physical or emotional effort. There is an immediate feeling of thankfulness, and a realisation that the earlier angst was pointless. I need to learn that finding what matters does not always require searching. It is there if I open my eyes. There will be moments, I hope, when life begins to make sense, but I have to accept that may happen when I least expect it.

The deeper things of life are the most difficult to see, and then to hold on to. To pursue them I need mental strength to understand them. I need to avoid being distracted by the inadequacies and failures of daily life. To cling to what I know is not the way to discover what I don't know.

Second Sunday of Easter

Beyond Doubt

Psalm 16 I Peter 1:3–9

Acts 2:14a, 22–32 John 20: 19-end

You have not seen him, yet you love him; and trusting in him now without seeing him, you are filled with a glorious joy too great for words, while you are reaping the harvest of your faith, that is salvation for your souls.

1 Peter 1:8–9

One of the Twelve, Thomas the Twin, was not with the rest when Jesus came. So the others kept telling him, 'We have seen the Lord.' But he said, 'Unless I see the mark of the nails on his hands, unless I put my finger into the place where the nails were, and my hand into his side I will never believe it.'

John 20:24–25

Although the doors were locked, Jesus came and stood among them, saying 'Peace be with you!' Then he said to Thomas, 'Reach you finger here; look at my hands. Reach you hand here and put it into my side. Be unbelieving no longer, but believe.' Thomas said, 'My Lord and my God.' Jesus said to him, 'Because you have seen me you have found faith. Happy are they who find faith without seeing me.'

John 20:26–29

I AM THOMAS. HE has always been given the dismissive name of Doubting Thomas. The other disciples believed what they thought they had seen. Thomas needed harder evidence. There has always been the feeling that this was a failure. Thomas lacked the faith, or the insight, or the trust of the other disciples, and so is set apart from them, to enjoy a story all his own. I am with Thomas all the way. However much I want the extraordinary to happen, however much I hope against hope that something will happen, when it does I am more likely to question it than jump for joy.

In the church calendar the readings for the Sundays after Easter describe the times Jesus appeared to his disciples after his death. It is difficult to know how to read them. Are they imaginative ghost stories, psychological explorations, literary wish fulfilment, or allegories of hope? The story that stands out from them all is Thomas' experience.

Other occasions are characterised by a preliminary non-recognition, followed by amazed acknowledgment that this is indeed Jesus. In Mary's story, outside the tomb, she is given a specific instruction not to touch, to accept that his presence is not real in any human sense. In Thomas' story Jesus appears magically, is instantly recognised, and has a presence that allows and requires physical contact with his wounds. This morbid fascinations with the cause of Jesus' painful death is as difficult for us to read as it must have been for Thomas to perform. It is not surprising that his doubt evaporates instantly.

It seems reasonable to assume that Thomas was not an isolated example of doubt and incredulity about the resurrection. It is difficult to believe that all the disciples and others who were close to Jesus instantly accepted the absolute truth that he had physically reappeared. So is the story of Thomas an exemplar of a more widespread doubt, with universal and personal significance?

Thomas saw and touched the wounds in Jesus' hands and side. We are told that was the moment his belief in the reality of the resurrection started. We are not told what he did next. We can assume that on his later travels, he preached with passion and conviction arising from his experiences. Was his experience convincing or just remarkable? The difficulty is always to make other people understand why something that is profoundly important to me should be important to them. Explaining what happened is just the start. Evidence is not enough.

This is the problem with much preaching is that it is "preaching to the converted." If congregations know the stories, have the Biblical "evidence" for their faith in their hearts and minds, if they believe they believe, what do they need to be told? A reiteration of home truths is comforting but not challenging. The repeated performance of ritual becomes a forgettable reminder. Anything that moves beyond the pleasure of a weekly meeting with friends is felt to be intrusive. Thomas gets a bad press because those who hear his story think they are not like him. The meaning of his story is that doubt matters because it gives depth to belief.

The story of Thomas is convincing as a story. It has tension, development, surprise, climax, and a moral. The question is, as always, what do I do with it? The sting in the tail is that while Jesus welcomes Thomas' new understanding he emphasises the happiness of those who reach the same understanding without physical evidence, a point repeated in the First Letter of Peter. This makes me uncomfortable. I cannot see the virtue in blind faith.

I am not looking for some kind of physical experience of God to give me confidence in what I believe. I do not want incontrovertible evidence that all the stories in the New Testament are true. I do not want anthropological and historical analysis that asserts our natural inclination to look for a Higher Being. In fact, I would be suspicious of, and would seriously doubt, all those.

I am seeking ways to look beyond the immediate, beyond the presenting problem, to something that is beyond doubt. Not in the sense that it is totally believable, but in the sense that it makes the doubting irrelevant.

I want to find and treasure the things in life (because that is all I have to work with) that make me see beyond the obvious, that suggest that there is more to life that meets the eye, that offer me glimmers of new understanding. I know that this will all be hesitant footsteps in a foggy night, with indistinct lights somewhere far ahead. I know that I will want clarity, and not find it. I know also that there will be moments, just moments, when life feels unspeakably good. It is in those moments that doubt ceases to matter.

Third Sunday of Easter
Excited Understanding

Psalm 116:1–7   1 Peter 1:17–23
Acts 2:14a, 36–41   Luke 24:13–35

(Peter) pressed his case with many other arguments and pleaded with them: 'Save yourselves from this crooked age.' Those who accepted what he said were baptized, and some three thousand were added to the number of believers that day.

Acts 2:40–41

Two of them were on their way to a village called Emmaus, about seven miles from Jerusalem, talking together about all that had happened. As they talked and argued, Jesus himself came up and walked with them, but something prevented them from recognising him.

Luke 24:13–16

When he had sat down with them at table, he took bread and said the blessing; he broke the bread and offered it to them. Then their eyes were opened, and they recognised him; but he vanished from their sight. They said one to another, 'Were not our hearts on fire as he talked with us on the road and explained the scriptures to us?'

Luke 24:30–32

IN THE STORIES OF Jesus' appearances after the crucifixion the Gospel writers continue to give him an intriguing personality. On the road to Emmaus Jesus feigns ignorance of current events to draw out a conversation with two of the disciples to find how much they understood about his death and resurrection. He expresses frustration, *"How dull you are!"*—at their lack of understanding, and then proceeds to put them right, but it is not until they sit down to a meal at the end of the day that they recognise him.

There is a wry humour here that is rare in the accounts of Jesus' life. Modest subterfuge seems uncharacteristic of him, but it is means to an important end. It gives Jesus the opportunity to explain how his life connects with everything that the disciples have been brought up to believe. Perhaps for the very first time, they understood, and were inspired—*"Were not our hearts on fire?"*

The nature of Jesus' appearance remains a mystery. At the start of the story he simply *came up and walked with them*, but at the end of the story, as soon as they recognised him *he vanished from their sight*. Even the writer of Luke's Gospel is perplexed. He has heard the story from others, but is still not sure what is going on—*something prevented them from recognising him*. Was it their own blindness and self-absorption, or did Jesus not want to be recognised until much later? Who knows?

Jesus' frustration was no doubt increased by their unabashed statement that they *"had been hoping that he was to be the liberator of Israel."* He must have wondered whether all his preaching and teaching had been worth it if they still believed that his earthly purpose was political revolution.

The same writer in the Acts of the Apostles adopts a different viewpoint. Any inadequacies in the disciples' understanding is now transformed in the powerful preaching of their successors leading to mass conversions. Peter's preaching was clearly passionate and convincing, focusing on the iniquities of the time rather than the spiritual failings of the populace. What he said made sense as an escape from *this crooked age* and thus inspired acceptance and commitment.

These contrasting stories seem to me to epitomise two different paths to belief and ways of believing, historical exemplars and moral uncertainty.

For the disciples it was a case of historical and literary explanation, drawing on an established canon of belief, making sense of prophecies, and clarifying truths that had hitherto seemed obscure. Jesus helped the disciples see his life and their lives in a new context, that validated everything he had done, everything he was, and everything they would be. For me, two thousand years later, it is difficult to disengage entirely from Christian history and Christian writing, to ignore cathedrals and religious art, to be deaf to choral music, to turn my back on the practical faith of millions of people. No matter how inadequate my own faith and belief, this wider context demands that I ask why Christianity has stood the test of time.

The twenty-first century is as *"crooked"* as any other. Some would argue more so, but how do they judge? I am sure that the declining power of the church, any church, as a force for good in society, the challenges of other faiths, the importance of diversity, differing moral imperatives, and the ambiguities of liberal thinking, set against the horrors of all wars, poverty, child abuse, starvation, excess, and exploitation of all kinds, give me, and I suspect many others, a longing for a raft of belief to hang on to, lest we drown.

The causal connection between strong preaching and a new acceptance of the Christian faith, or any faith for that matter, seems too simplistic to me, though history suggests otherwise. There have been many preachers who in their time converted thousands, inspired "revivals", and filled their churches, rooms or even fields with those eager to hear what they had to say.

Evangelists of all persuasions have filled stadia and commanded huge television audiences. However, it is not the numbers that matter. This is something entirely individual for people who in their own way, in their own time, in their own lives, found a new understanding of life that made sense.

The disciples were inspired by what Jesus said to them, but it took some time for it all to sink in. My Methodist upbringing reminds me that according to his Journal, the turning point in John Wesley's life was when he "reluctantly" attended a church meeting in Aldersgate and, echoing the disciples on the Emmaus road, his heart was "strangely warmed" by what he heard. He gained a new understanding of what he believed.

I believe that understanding requires a slow and often reluctant awareness and recognition of hitherto half-acknowledged truths, but for that understanding to grow and last I need to be excited by it.

Fourth Sunday of Easter

Herd Instincts

Psalm 23   1 Peter 2:19–end
Acts 2:42–end   John 10:1–11

The Lord is my shepherd; I lack for nothing. He makes me lie down in green pastures, he leads me to water where I may rest; he revives my spirit; for his name's sake he guides me in the right paths.

PSALM 23:1

He carried our sins in his own person on the gibbet, so that we might cease to live for sin and begin to live for righteousness. By his wounds you have been healed. You were straying like sheep, but now you have turned towards the Shepherd and Guardian of your souls.

I PETER 2:24–25

I am the door of the sheepfold. The sheep paid no heed to any who came before me, for they were all thieves and robbers. I am the door; anyone who comes into the fold through me will be safe. He will go in and out and find pasture. A thief comes only to steal, kill and destroy; I have come that they may have life, and may have it in all its fullness. I am the good shepherd; the good shepherd lays down his life for his sheep.

JOHN 10:7–11

The imagery of shepherd and sheep is easy to understand though time has eroded its immediacy. The picture is now tinted with the rosy romanticism of a times gone by, ignoring the harsh realities of a shepherd's life. At the same time, for humanity to be compared to or described as sheep now has such pejorative associations—silly, timid, gullible, frightened, unthinking, following each other—that the image is more likely to cause offence than aid understanding.

It now seems an aberration to use these traditional images from the New Testament as a way in to understanding the relevance of Christ's teaching today. They have a sentimental attraction but no real relation to modern life. Psalm 23 is one of the most well-known of all the Psalms but is now no more than romantic poetry. The shepherd does not ring true as an exemplar of a caring leader, and dying to defend a herd of sheep seems misguided.

No matter how anachronistic the imagery may be, its very simplicity sticks in the mind. Are we therefore lulled into acceptance by the poetry, ignoring current connotations in pursuit of a pastoral idyll, accepting its meaning at face value, in fact behaving like sheep? The implication that we all share the same characteristics as an unthinking and timid herd, misses the point of who and what we are. We certainly share a common need for the water, food, and shelter, but beyond subsistence our needs are very different.

Jesus describes himself as someone who helps everyone find spiritual safety, sustenance, and achieve a full and meaningful life. He echoes the Psalmist who thanks God for giving him support and guidance in both good times and bad throughout his life. My question, to myself, is, do I have to believe that he will do this before I can see that he does, or do I have to behave like a sheep and follow the Christian herd?

I have been told frequently from the pulpit that the church is the people in it, not the building they sit in. I can understand the importance of community, friendship, and mutual support as a direct expression of Christian ideals, but I am worried that "going to church" often feels nothing like that. Many churches are rightly criticised for being cold, unwelcoming, and too locked up in their own internal affairs and conflicts. That behaviour neither encourages nor enhances belief.

Assuming, charitably, that such churches are in the minority, I ask myself whether a caring and supportive congregation does indeed promote belief and spiritual understanding. If everyone appears to believe in what they are doing in church, does that give confidence to the more uncertain and wavering that belief itself comes from being part of that community? Are there positive benefits from a herd mentality of this kind? I am not sure, and I wait to be convinced.

I know that I am part of the common herd, but if I want to preserve my individuality and gain an understanding of my unique place and purpose in the world I need to look beyond the foibles and vagaries of human nature. Belonging to a group does not mean that we like or feel kinship with every member of it. We do not let our feelings show (if we want our membership of the group to last), and we try to see the best in people. This is not easy. We need guidance, encouragement, and words of understanding. I worry that the legacy of the shepherd is no longer engaging the attention of the sheep.

Jesus' teaching offers a way in to thinking about the world and life *"in all its fullness"* and for vast numbers of Christians, now and then, this does indeed offer a sense of security and the spiritual food that they need. Not everyone is so lucky. Preachers and evangelists have a conviction that the truths they preach will change hearts and minds, but they use concepts that are difficult to follow. The words in the First Letter of Peter, *"He carried our sins in his own person"* and *"By his wounds you have been healed"* are the common currency of church discourse, but they are alien to my normal thinking and need reinterpretation before they can be valuable. I do not know where they are leading me, and I am still wandering, as I believe are many others like me.

For me the message of the shepherd and the sheep needs updating to focus on a new relationship between those who act as spiritual shepherds and the needs of their flock. Those needs are disparate and often desperate. They need personal attention and support that is as hard to find in the *"sheepfold"* of the church as it is in society as a whole. The door may be open, but not many are coming. Does the problem lie with the shepherd or the sheep?

Fifth Sunday of Easter
Paths to Truth

Psalm 32 I Peter 2:2–10
Acts 7:55–end John 14:1–14

'There are many dwelling places in my Father's house; if it were not so I should have told you; for I am going to prepare a place for you. And if I go and prepare a place for you, I shall come again to take you to myself, so that where I am going you may be also; and you know the way I am taking.'

JOHN 14:2–4

Thomas said, 'Lord, we do not know where you are going, so how can we know the way?' Jesus replied, 'I am the way, the truth and the life; no one comes to the Father except by me. If you knew me you would know my Father too. From now on you do know him; you have seen him.'

JOHN 14:5–7

Philip said to him, 'Lord, show us the Father; we ask no more.' Jesus answered, 'Have I been all this time with you, Philip, and you still do not know me. Anyone who has seen me has seen the Father. Then how can you say "Show us the Father"? Do you not believe that I am in the Father, and the Father in me?

JOHN 14:8–10

THE ONLY WAY WE can think about the next life is to use ideas from this life. These ideas are inevitably inappropriate to a state of being that we cannot begin to imagine. The closest we can get is a world in which physical attributes are merged with emotional contentment as in a dream. The feeling of what it might be makes it what it is. Jesus has the same problem. The words he has to use cannot do justice to what he is describing but he has to use them all the same.

The sentence *'There are many dwelling places in my Father's house'* has encouraged many different interpretations. Other translations replace *'dwelling places'* with 'rooms' or 'mansions', two extremes of a heavenly estate agent's description, but these do little to clarify the meaning. Leaving all my other doubts aside, I have never had any difficulty with this. It seems to me that if Jesus was on earth to be an exemplar to us all, and to encourage new thinking about the meaning of life now and the meaning of life after we die, that message in the first instance must be for everyone.

None of us are denied the spiritual opportunities Jesus presents to us. It is our own behaviour that puts barriers in the way of full understanding or enjoyment. Jesus is saying that the divisions of status, education, wealth, faith, and religious practice that bedevil us here have no meaning or relevance after death. His message is very practical. If there were such divisions he would have explained this to the disciples so that they could do something about it in their own lives, now. The immediate requirement is to understand what he has to say, and follow him. There lies the problem for the disciples, and us. The clarity and simplicity of what he is saying is lost on them because they cannot look beyond the present.

Thomas and Philip voice their perplexity. As has happened so often on other occasions, Jesus finds their lack of understanding frustrating. We may think that he might have been more understanding about their lack of understanding, but his time was running out. He needed to get his message across so that the disciples themselves had a solid foundation for their own preaching and teaching. At the moment, in John's account, they are all on shaky intellectual and spiritual ground. They are not alone.

Thomas' approach is practical. He wants to know where Jesus is going so that he can take the necessary steps, literally and metaphorically to follow him. Thomas is purposeful and focused on the process necessary to get him where he wants to be. I can empathise with him. He finds it uncomfortable that Jesus is asking him to think in a different way.

Philip is more visionary. He believes that Jesus has the power to reveal God to the disciples. Like Philip I would like to have a clear, or at least clearer, understanding of the nature of God. All the attempts I make are deeply unsatisfactory, and I envy those who have a clearer vision than I do. Philip wants this clarity to be immediate. That will be enough. Jesus challenges him to think differently. What Philip is looking for he has already seen. Do I have to look in a different way?

'*I am the way, the truth, and the life*' has become a Christian mantra that deserves deep meditation. Jesus clarifies these words by adding, '*No one comes to the Father except by me*'. Like Thomas and Philip I am just beginning to appreciate fully what he meant. To understand Jesus is to have an understanding of God. This however is not a purely intellectual exercise. There are three elements, distinct yet interwoven.

Jesus' life, in all its complexity, happiness, and pain is a model for us to follow, but not an easy one. I need to transfer the moral standards from one age to another, and still find them relevant. I need to recognize the current validity of Jesus' intolerance with hypocrisy in secular and religious life. I need to emulate his concern for the rejected and marginalised. I need to respond to the challenges he offers to my faltering understanding. I need to find the truth in what he said and did.

Finding the truth is an intellectual exercise, but one that only makes sense in the context of my life, and the world in which I live. That life and that world are full of contradictions, ambiguities, false hopes, false starts, horrific mistakes, small achievements, good and bad relationships, much happiness, some despair, great expectations, and faltering hope. Making sense of all that is difficult.

Understanding the deeper meanings of life is only possible if we have a moral path and profound truths to follow. I am surprised to admit that Jesus offers both those.

Sixth Sunday of Easter
Groping in the Dark

Psalm 66:7–end   I Peter 3:13–end
Acts 17:22–31   John 14:15–21

He created from one stock every nation of men to inhabit the whole earth's surface. He determined their eras in history and the limits of their territory. They were to seek God in the hope that, groping after him, they might find him; though indeed he is not far from each one of us, for in him we live and move, in him we exist.

Acts 17:26–28

If you love me you will obey my commands; and I will ask the Father, and he will give you another to be your advocate, who will be with you for ever—the Spirit of Truth. The world cannot accept him, because the world neither sees nor knows him; but you know him because he dwells with you and will be in you.

John 14:15–17

In a little while the world will see me no longer, but you will see me; because I live you too will live. When that day comes you will know that I am in my Father, and you in me and I in you. Anyone who has received my commands and obeys them—he it is who loves me, and he who loves me will be loved by my Father; and I will love him and disclose myself to him.

John 14:19–21

To look for a relevant, personal message in these Bible passages leads to a collision of ideas. On the one hand there is much to reject, on the other much to think about. Taken together I am left with a feeling that I half understand what the writers are saying but I could not explain why that is to anyone else. Is it the case that the more elusive the words, the more I cling on to them for deeper meaning? Do I over-intellectualise, turning a simple message into something obscure, thus defeating its object? Do ideas that feel true need explanation? This is difficult stuff to deal with.

It is easy to dismiss the creation story in chapter 17 of the Acts of the Apostles because it does not fit in with my current understanding of how the world began. I feel reasonably confident in saying that God's creative powers were not like that. Is that blasphemy, arrogance, or ignorance? I may be deluded in thinking that I understand God's actions, purpose and intentions, but before I can go any further the writer brings me down to earth with a statement that is startling modern. He says we are all here *to seek God in the hope that, groping after him,* we might find him. Groping after him! That is exactly what it feels like, in a darkness of uncertainty or in a fog of incomprehension. The writer then offers us new hope. We need to think about God in a new way as a spiritual being who is around us and part of us. We can stop groping. Or can we? Can I? I am not so sure.

My responses to the arguments in John's Gospel are similar, easy acceptance of the words, but a difficult struggle to understand their meaning, particularly *"He (the Father) will give you another to be your advocate, who will be with you for ever—the Spirit of Truth."* I am very familiar with the idea of the Trinity, God the Father, God the Son, and God the Holy Spirit, and I have been blessed in their name many times, without understanding the third member is important or necessary.

Once again we are using the words of the Bible to explain the unexplainable and to describe relationships that are indescribable because they are spiritual. If our whole understanding of God and Jesus is spiritual, what is the purpose of the Holy Spirit? Is it simply that the Gospel writers had devoted so much attention to the facts of Jesus' life on earth and his relationship with God, that reached its consummation after death, that they needed a new medium to carry Christ's message forward?

If that is the case the *Spirit of Truth* becomes a way of describing how we think about the unthinkable, imagine the unimaginable, and pursue a relationship with the unknowable. In that context we have the paradox that the *Truth* we are seeking is unknowable because it is impossible to find. More convinced Christian believers than I am will argue that it is faith that will give us the confidence that truth can be found, making the accumulation of impossibilities irrelevant. I remain unconvinced, except for one assurance.

John recognises that the *Spirit of Truth* is something personal—*You know him because he dwells with you and will be in you.* It is my understanding of what all this means to me that makes it truth. My understanding, my truth, may not be the same as anyone else's, but because we are all seeking to understand the deeper mysteries of life, we are all part of the same exploration. We have much to learn from each other. My indecision and questioning may be another's revelation. Another's certainty may prompt my questioning.

All this may focus attention on verbal and intellectual contradictions, but John makes it clear that knowledge of God comes through an obedience to Jesus' message that grows out of love not obligation. Love is an acceptance of contradictions. Love is a new understanding of self through understanding another. Love is believing that it all makes sense. Love is a vision of good that goes beyond immediate problems. That suggests to me that the more profound is my acceptance of Jesus' message, the more profound will be my understanding of its meaning for me.

This is not, however, blind or unquestioning acceptance. How can it be? The ideas are complex, the moral code challenging, the impact on society revolutionary, universal acceptance unachievable, and the personal demands huge. I need to accept the reality of a spiritual guide that will help me grope through these fogs of doubt and the mists of obscurity, towards some kind of truth.

Ascension Day

Rising to New Heights

Psalm 47   Ephesians 1:15–end
Acts 1:1–11   Luke 24:44–end

He was lifted up before their very eyes, and a cloud took him from their sight. They were gazing intently into the sky as he went, and all at once there stood beside them two men robed in white, who said, 'Men of Galilee, why stand there looking up into the sky? This Jesus who has been taken from you up to heaven will come in the same way as you have seen him go.'

ACTS 1:9–11

I pray that the God of our Lord Jesus Christ, the all-glorious Father, may confer on you the spiritual gifts of wisdom and vision, with the knowledge of him that they bring. I pray that your inward eyes may be enlightened, so that you may know the hope to which he calls you.

EPHESIANS 1:17–18

Then he led them out as far as Bethany, and blessed them with uplifted hands; and in the act of blessing he parted from them. And they returned to Jerusalem full of joy, and spent all their time in the temple praising God.

LUKE 24:50–53

Ascension is one of the five great feasts of the Christian church and one of the most difficult to comprehend and celebrate. New Testament cosmography—up to heaven, down to hell—does not translate into modern thinking, even though we still use that directional language.

So what am I going to make of the stories of Christ's "ascent to heaven"?

It is very easy to accept that the writer of Luke's Gospel and of the Acts of the Apostles was doing his best to put into words the disciples' spiritual and metaphysical experience that marked the end of Jesus' post-death appearances to them. They no longer needed to puzzle over the meaning of the resurrection, or stretch their imaginations to embrace the idea that Christ was still with them. That experience was now part of their lives and of their teaching. The next stage was to change perspective and think of Jesus Christ as one with God, just as he had always taught them he is, was and would be. That was then, what about now?

For me there are two sentences in the verses above that give me a way in to understanding the meaning of the Ascension today. First of all, the disciples *"returned to Jerusalem full of joy."* Their experience of the Ascension was not a sad one. They were losing Jesus for a second time, which we might consider particularly painful after the horrors of the crucifixion and the joy of the resurrection, but they were very happy. This was the moment when they realised that Christ would indeed by always with them as his form and substance had changed. If that seems a naïve and mechanistic interpretation, the second passage from Acts is helpful.

In the first chapter of Acts *two men robed in white* appear to the disciples immediately after Jesus, we are told, disappeared in a cloud. Angelic beings in the New Testament are always very forthright in their manner and speech. There is nothing ethereal in what they say. They come straight to the point and ask why the disciples are gazing, probably open mouthed, at the sky: *"This Jesus who has been taken from you up to heaven will come in the same way as you have seen him go."* This miraculous departure is for them just the precursor of a second coming some time, somewhere. That was something they could immediately look forward to. It is not surprising that they were *full of joy.* For me there is new hope in believing that just as the Ascension was a mystery fabricated into a story, a second coming, or new realisation of Christ's presence, will be equally mysterious and require a story to explain it.

I have no more time for the notion that Jesus disappeared in a cloud than I have for the idea that angels appeared to the disciples and made them see things in a new way. Once again the story can get in the way of its interpretation. For me the story of the Ascension, coming at the end of all the stories about Christ's life on earth, is part of an unfolding metaphor of how I might approach the Christian faith.

It starts with the birth of an idea, unexpected, perhaps unwanted, full of threats and contradictions. This idea is strengthened by the supportive belief of others, and their convictions that this idea is something important and life changing.

As the idea gains hold and credibility I want to become involved with and accepted by others of the same persuasion. This involves a small ritual, an initiation ceremony that requires statements of commitment by myself and others on my behalf. My ideas now have a new context and community.

It is not plain sailing from there. Initial confidence is dented by doubt. The community begins to feel alien, and its teaching remote. The language promotes the idea of new revelations, but the world seems to get in the way. There is an undertow that pulls me back, and the wind always seems to be blowing against me rather than behind me. Quite suddenly the effort seems pointless.

What follows is a death of faith. A painful death that requires a dismissal (if not complete rejection) of many ideas and beliefs that I have held dear for most of my life. There is nothing in their place, and far from feeling released and relieved, I feel abandoned.

Later, much later, new experiences, new friends, new reading, new thinking bring about a small resurrection of the ideas I had earlier dismissed. I am reluctant to admit this. Sometimes the resurrected ideas are clear and helpful. At other times they are dark and obscure. I need clarity, but I cannot find it.

My hope is that eventually there will come a moment when my thinking rises to new heights that transcend the doubts and I overcome the things that hinder my belief.

Seventh Sunday of Easter / Sunday after Ascension Day

Humble Knowledge

Psalm 68:1–10, 32–35 I Peter 4:12–14; 5:6–11

Acts 1:6–14 John 17:1–11

You should all clothe yourselves with humility towards one another, because 'God sets his face against the arrogant but shows favour to the humble'. Humble yourselves, then, under God's mighty hand, and in due time he will lift you up. He cares for you, so cast all your anxiety on him.

1 Peter 5:5–6

Be on the alert! Wake up! Your enemy the devil, like a roaring lion, prowls around looking for someone to devour. Stand up to him, firm in your faith, and remember that your fellow Christians in this world are going through the same kinds of suffering.

1 Peter 5:8–9

'I have made your name known to the men whom you gave me out of the world. They were yours and you gave them to me, and they have obeyed your command. Now they know that all you gave me has come from you; for I have taught them what I learned from you, and they have received it: they know with certainty that I came from you, and they have believed that you sent me.'

John 17:6–8

HUMBLE KNOWLEDGE

AFTER THE ASCENSION, THE writer of the Acts of the Apostles tells us that the disciples returned to Jerusalem and went to the upstairs room where they were staying. They were all there, Peter, John, James, Andrew, Philip, Thomas, Bartholomew, Matthew, James son of Alphaeus, Simon the Zealot, and Judas son of James, together with *a group of women, and Mary, the mother of Jesus, and his brothers.* This was an important moment. Jesus' closest followers and his family came together to pray, take stock of their situation, and plan for the future.

Jesus had told the disciples: *'Go therefore to all nations and make them my disciples; baptise them in the name of the Father, the Son and the Holy Spirit, and teach them to observe all that I have commanded you.'* (Matthew 28:19–20) They were now faced with the enormous challenges of how to respond to this command.

It is helpful to find common ground with their situation and learn something from it that may illuminate my own. The three passages above highlight four important issues for me: aptitude, knowledge, humility, and fear.

The disciples were not educated men. Using today's parlance, they were trusting, honourable, in touch with the needs of the peers, alert to the customs and practices of their day, God-fearing, church going, and committed to the path they had chosen. They had all given up jobs and careers to follow Jesus, driven by something they had yet to discover, for a purpose as yet unclear. They were an elite band.

The verses from John emphasise that Jesus had chosen to work through men that God had helped him identify as right for the job. Today we might say Jesus selected them for attitude and behaviour, rather than skills and expertise. He never patronised them, or talked down to them, he trained them. He was certainly frustrated by their lack of understanding from time to time, and said so, but in the end he was convinced that they understood who he was, why he lived, and why he died, and were ready to spread that message worldwide.

Only a few of us are called to be priests, ministers, pastors and evangelists, but I believe that each of us has the potential to be chosen for some task that helps spread an understanding of the things that matter in life. There is however a very real danger in saying or suggesting that "I know something that could help you." That sounds arrogant, patronising, and demeaning. It is the downfall of those who claim to have privileged access to Christian truth. They may be extremely charismatic, great preachers, and buoyant in prayer, but their assumption of superior knowledge will drive people away in the end. The First Letter of Peter warns against this by advocating great humility, and that is a message that is as important now as it was then.

I do not believe that this means a shy, retiring, self-effacing approach to life and relationships with others. That is the kind of humility that removes personality. For me it is the humility that identifies with others, that shares their difficulties, that explores problems openly, and draws out solutions rather than imposing them. This is good in theory, but opportunity is rare, and opposition common.

The early Christians were alive to the risks they ran and the very real dangers of persecution. I am equally alive to more insidious fears, prowling around in my mind: What is my role in spreading a message that I only half believe? Can I trust my own judgement when I am exploring ideas that greater minds than mine have wrestled with for over two thousand years? Am I confident that talking to people about spiritual ideas will help them and not drive them away, destroying any relationship we might have? How do I cope with the fact that many people hold beliefs, and practice their faith in ways that I instinctively reject? Do I have any right to burden others with my private doubts and difficulties? Can I make any claims to Christian belief if I have no time or inclination for Christian practice?

The passage from the First Letter of Peter gives some encouragement. I am not alone. Others are facing exactly the same fears and difficulties. But is this as encouraging as it sounds? How do I find them? Churches appear to operate a closed shop of certainty, where the collective will and concerted practice reject dissent, questioning, argument, and rejection. There are times when it seems as if there are more *roaring lions* in the pews than there are outside.

The final sentence of this passage is all important to me. We are all in the hands of God (though I may have difficulty coming to terms with what that means) and we can "cast our anxiety on him." For me that means being honest about all these difficulties, with the humble belief that I will sooner or later reach unexpected conclusions and resolutions.

Day of Pentecost/Whit Sunday
Varieties of Gifts

Psalm 104:26–end   1 Corinthians 12:3b–13
Acts 2:1–21   John 7:37–39

The Day of Pentecost has come, and they were all together in one place. Suddenly there came from the sky what sounded like a strong, driving wind, a noise which filled the whole house where they were sitting. And there appeared to them flames like tongues of fire distributed among them and coming to rest on each one. They were all filled with the Holy Spirit and began to talk in other tongues, as the Spirit gave them power of utterance.

ACTS 2:1–4

There are varieties of gifts, but the same Spirit. There are varieties of service, but the same Lord. There are varieties of activity, but in all of them and in everyone the same God is active. In each of us the Spirit is seen to be at work for some useful purpose.

1 CORINTHIANS 12:4–7

One, through the Spirit, has the gift of wise speech, while another, by the power of the same Spirit, can put the deepest knowledge into words. Another, by the same Spirit, is granted faith; another, by the one Spirit, gifts of healing, and another miraculous powers; another has the ability to distinguish true spirits from false; yet another has the gift of tongues of various kinds, and another the ability to interpret them.

1 CORINTHIANS 12:8–10

Pentecost marks the start of the disciples' ministry to the wider world, and therefore in the eyes of the Christian church its own birth. Pentecost is an iconic moment. It is dramatic and life changing for the disciples who experienced wind and fire and found an ability to speak other languages. What can we make of it?

Some people regard "speaking in tongues" as a real spiritual gift. I cannot understand what that means or how it works. I can understand this story as a way of describing the discovery of new powers of communication. I see it as a way of explaining a sudden inspiration, an extraordinary growth in confidence. At this moment the disciples found in themselves an ability to communicate that hitherto they did not think they had. Not only did they find new words to put their message across, but they discovered that their audience had a new understanding of what they were saying. This was a revelation and therefore the true start of their ministry.

This story is coupled with Paul's First Letter to the Corinthians in which he offers important guidance for anyone thinking about any kind of ministry, exploring how their own skills and talents can be of value. Paul emphasises that we all have something to offer, and all our gifts have a common origin and purpose. He lists nine gifts. It is easy to find modern equivalents for most of these, but some need further thought.

He starts with *wise speech*, an essential gift for any preacher. The wisdom lies not just what is said, but how it is said. This is the wisdom of knowing your audience, tailoring words to their needs and expectations, and helping their understanding. This must be coupled with the second gift, the ability to *put the deepest knowledge into words*. Jesus had left a legacy of complex ideas and challenges to the way we think about our lives, our behaviour and society as a whole, all growing out of unequivocal belief in God and the reality of his spiritual presence with us all. This was difficult for the disciples to understand then, and remains so for us today. It is therefore essential that those with the responsibility or the desire to explain the Christian faith can unpack the most profound ideas and put them across in ways that engage hearts and minds. Sadly, this is a rarity.

The third gift, *faith,* is surprising. It is reasonable to believe that all those involved in the early days of the church had faith. It is more prudent to recognise that we are all different. Some of us will have a more profound faith than others. This was true of the disciples, who expressed their own doubts and uncertainties, so why should it not be true of us. Faith is difficult. Faith is often tenuous. Faith is a struggle. To preach faith, we need faith. It is an important gift to find and hold on to.

Did Paul include *healing* and *miraculous powers* in his list from wishful thinking, or a real belief that the disciples would be blessed with the same abilities as Jesus? Jesus had led the disciples to believe that, but would their faith be strong enough to make it a reality? Today, there are indeed people who appear to have healing powers, and miracles do appear to happen. Who am I to doubt them, but I interpret these gifts in a more downbeat way. We all have difficulties and problems in our lives and we experience pain and unhappiness of many kinds. We need to find people who can help us resolve these and offer us healing support. When the pain and unhappiness lifts it may well seem miraculous because we could not have imagined it. People who can help us in this way have a great gift.

Prophecy is not, to my mind, the ability to see into the future. It means to understand what might be. To describe, from experience, how events may turn out if certain actions are taken, or if a particular behaviour pattern continues, and to advise and guide accordingly. We are all prone to reject or ignore such advice. We think we know better. All too often the advice we reject turns out to be the advice we should have followed.

Paul includes the ability to *distinguish true spirits from false* in his list. For me this is distinguishing between teaching and advice that is truly helpful, and not just superficially attractive. We all need to recognise this ability in ourselves before we can begin to help others.

Finally, Paul lists *tongues of various kinds* and *interpretation*. We must cultivate the ability to speak in a language that is appropriate to our audience. We must also actively listen, so that our interpretation and understanding is truly based on what they say, not on our view of the world which may not be theirs.

Varied as these gifts are, and varied as we are, they will help our purpose in life, even if we do not understand what that is.

Trinity Sunday
What About God?

Isaiah 40:12–17, 27–end   2 Corinthians 13:11–end
Psalm 8   Matthew 28:16–20

Who has measured the waters of the sea in the hollow of his hand, or with its span gauged the heavens? Who has held all the soil of the earth in a bushel? Or weighed the mountains on a balance, the hills on a pair of scales? Who has directed the spirit of the Lord? What counsellor stood at his side to instruct him? With whom did he confer to gain discernment? Who taught him this path of justice or taught him knowledge, or showed him the way of wisdom? To him the nations are but drops from a bucket, no more than moisture on the scales; to him coasts and islands weigh as light as specks of dust.

Isaiah 40:12–15

When I look up at your heavens, the work of your fingers, at the moon and the stars you have set in place, what is a frail mortal, that you should be mindful of him, a human being, that you should take notice of him?

Psalm 8:3–4

Jesus came near and said to them: 'Full authority in heaven and on earth has been committed to me. Go therefore to all nations and

> *make them my disciples, baptize them in the name of the Father and the Son and the Holy Spirit, and teach them to observe all that I have commanded you. I will be with you always, to the end of time.*
>
> MATTHEW 28:18–20

WHAT DO I DO about God? Believe in him because not believing is impossible, or not believe in him because believing is impossible? Talk about him using analogies and metaphors that stretch language to its limits, and still feel inadequate? Argue the finer points of eternity, heaven, creation, the trinity, as if they were measurable realities? Find a new God pronoun that avoids gender? Assign to God personal characteristics that reflect the best in us, even though that limits him to what we are? Deny vehemently the vengeful and authoritarian God of the Old Testament, but fail to define the nature of God's power? Accept the truth of Jesus, but wonder why God would do it that way? Deride theological arguments that assume a belief in order to explain what that belief is? Or admit with confidence that a few bars of beautiful music, lines of poetry, words in a speech, crashing waves, pictures from deep space, the birth of a baby, a novel, a sunset, or a moment of passionate love can lift my spirits to a point when I say, this goes beyond what I understand but I believe this is where God is.

Isaiah was facing the same problem. The only difference was that he knew what he believed about God but had to find ways of describing the infinite and the ultimate. It is a truly great passage. Isaiah believes that God is greater than anything, with a wisdom that began before knowledge. To God we are *no more than moisture on the scales,* (in some translations we are merely specks of dust), almost invisible, evaporating in seconds, easy to wipe away, almost an irrelevance. The Psalmist has the same feeling: *What is a frail mortal that you should be mindful of him, a human being, that you should take notice of him.* Then he goes on to express his amazement and gratitude that we have been created at all:

> *Yet you have made him little less than a god, crowning his head with glory and honour. You make him master over all that you have made, putting everything in subjection under his feet: all sheep and oxen, all the wild beasts, the birds in the air, the fish in the sea, and everything that moves along ocean paths.*—Psalm 8:5–8

Isaiah too moves from an evocation of God's magnitude to a poetic statement of his personal involvement with all of us:

> *He gives vigour to the weary, new strength to the exhausted. Young men may grow weary and faint, even the fittest may stumble and fall; but those who look to the Lord will win new strength, they will soar as on eagles' wings; they will run and not feel faint, march on and not grow weary.*—Isaiah 40:29–31

Our creative ingenuity never stops. Our knowledge continues to grow. Our understanding of the nature of life expands daily. There is no end in sight to what we can know and what we need to know. We are part of an infinite creation. Is that where God is?

Creation for its own sake has no point. It is we who make sense of what creation is and what it is for. It is, I believe, God in us that gives meaning to what we are and why we are here. We may live for only eight or nine decades, a mere nothing, but in that short time create life, discover new things, bring happiness, wipe away tears, comfort and care for others, solve problems, do what we can to remove the worst aspects of our society. That is what we are here for. That makes sense of creation to me. Can I believe that is what God wants?

I want to believe that God is the spirit of love and goodness that is in us all. I want to believe that in ways I cannot understand he is to be found as much in the most beautiful things of life as in pain and suffering. I want to believe that the unexpected can reveal new truths. I want to believe that the nature of belief is nothing more than a glimmer of light from the other end of the universe, but none the less real. I want to believe that the one part of me that cannot be measured is the spiritual essence that makes me what I am. I want to believe that my conscious lack of faith is the path to faith. Does wanting make it so?

Jesus gave the disciples a new way to think about God as Father, Son, and Holy Spirit. This trinity of names prevents us falling into the trap of personalising God and making him in our image. To suggest that God "wants" anything, or "dislikes" anything, or "chooses" anything misses the point. He is part of us because we are his creation. He is us, and we are him because it is through us that his creation is made real.

Jesus instructed his disciples to help the world, and that means us, understand our spiritual and moral responsibilities to create a world whose the purpose is self-evident because, in the words of Genesis, *God saw that it was good.* He is the good that we see.

First Sunday after Trinity
Losing and Finding

Jeremiah 20:7–13   Romans 6:1b–11
Psalm 69:14–20   Matthew 10:24–39

Whenever I said, 'I shall not call to mind or speak his name again,' then his word became imprisoned within me like a fire burning in my heart. I was weary with holding it under, and could endure no more.

Jeremiah 20:9

'Are not two sparrows sold for a penny? Yet without your Father's knowledge not one of them can fall to the ground. As for you, even the hairs on your head have all been counted. So do not be afraid; you are worth more than any number of sparrows.'

Matthew 10:29–30

'No one is worthy of me who cares more for father or mother than for me; no one is worthy of me who cares more for son or daughter; no one is worthy of me who does not take up his cross and follow me. Whoever gains his life will lose it; whoever loses his life for my sake will gain it.'

Matthew 10:37–39

THE READINGS FOR THE previous Sunday contrast the enormity (if that is the right word) of God with the frailty of man, yet Isaiah and the Psalmist are amazed at the responsibilities that we have been given and the support that God gives us to carry them out. In these passages from Matthew Jesus gives a more personal slant to the same theme. God's omniscience is such that he is aware of everything and cares for everything. My understanding of this has nothing to do with God "looking down" on dead sparrows or watching the minutest details of our lives. God's involvement with us, and our involvement with him, is inevitable and unavoidable because he is part of everything. He knows us because he is us, whether we choose to acknowledge him or not.

If this leads to complacency, quiet spiritual contentment, or a laissez-faire attitude to religious belief, Jesus is quick to dispel any such thoughts. He speaks in words that are designed to shock, that go to the very foundation of society, the family:

> *'You must not think that I have come to bring peace to the earth; I have not come to bring peace, but a sword. I have come to set a man against his father, a daughter against her mother, a daughter-in-law against her mother-in-law; and a man will find his enemies under his own roof.'*—Matthew 10: 34–36

This may well be a fact of life if one member of any family chooses a path in life that is contrary to parental beliefs and customs. Jesus is not talking about a temperamental outburst or a wilful flouting of family mores. He is describing the unsettling result of a conscious choice that, initially at least, will cause dissent, anger and unhappiness. This is brutal realism.

I read this as an example of Jesus dramatically forcing the disciples, and therefore us, to face the realities of belief in a new world order. It is not just going to be difficult, it is going to require a reappraisal of everything that we hold dear. We have to decide where our priorities lie. Jesus does not want dilettante believers, cotton wool faith, or smug contentment. Revolutions do not happen that way. He demands firm choices, gritty determination, and serious heart-searching.

This is pulpit-thumping rhetoric that is not to everyone's taste. We may well say that we are not really faced with choices of that kind. Life is not so extreme. We struggle along but we are not in the business of "taking up crosses." We are not afraid to say that we are pretty content with being the caring, sharing Christians that we think we are. There is nothing intrinsically "wrong" with any of that, but Jesus seems to be saying that effort is required to really appreciate and live his message. Being a Christian is a lot harder than believing you are a Christian. That is why the passage ends with a paradox: *Whoever gains his life will lose it; whoever loses his life for my sake will gain it.*

I believe that Jesus is not talking about life-style choices, but an attitude of mind that will affect the way we live. This is not a parallel statement to "sell all you have and follow me." It is not a contrast between the material and the spiritual. It is an intellectual process, available to us all, whoever we are, whatever our aspirations. Jesus is saying that if we think we have all the answers, if we hang on to ideas that we grew up with, if we feel we have never had it so good, we will almost certainly be disappointed. On the other hand, if we fight against complacency and self-satisfaction, if we use his teaching as a vade mecum for our lives, then we will discover something new and life enhancing. The battles and conflicts will be internal, and painful. Our new thinking and behaviour may well cause us to fall out with people we hitherto called friends. This will be distressing and disheartening, but in the end, in ways we cannot imagine, it will all turn out to be the right thing to do.

Here and now, in the life that I live, in the middle of shopping in Tesco on a wet Monday morning in a cold January, this can seem simpering and sentimental, worse than pulpit thumping rhetoric. It smacks of the grinning evangelism. Irritating leaflets through the letterbox. Clean cut young men wanting to "talk about God." Moralistic exhortations to "rethink your life." All the trappings of smug religiosity that are alien to my way of thinking. As such it is all easy to reject, because "I have better things to do with my time." Then I am prompted to wonder, in the middle of the dog food aisle, whose time is it, and what would be better?

The unexpected impact of reading familiar passages from the New Testament afresh is that the more enigmatic and paradoxical are the words of Jesus, the more they stick in the mind. They are easy to dismiss, but they do not go away completely. Jeremiah, in the passage above, summed this up perfectly. The more he tried to reject thoughts about God, the more he found they stayed with him, until he was *weary with holding it under, and could endure no more.* Jesus is saying that if we lose our natural inclinations to stifle and reject unwelcome ideas, we will discover something of extraordinary value.

Second Sunday after Trinity
Prophets of Good

Jeremiah 28:5–9 Romans 6:12–23
Psalm 89:8–18 Matthew 10:40–end

'The prophets who preceded you and me from the earliest times have foretold war, famine, and pestilence for many lands and for great kingdoms. If a prophet foretells prosperity, it will be known that the Lord has sent him only when his words come true.'

Jeremiah 28:8–9

Sin must no longer reign in your mortal body, exacting obedience to the body's desires. You must no longer put any part of it at sin's disposal, as an implement for doing wrong. Put yourselves instead at the disposal of God; think of yourselves as raised from death to life, and yield your bodies to God as implements of doing right. Sin shall no longer be your master, for you are no longer under law, but under grace.

Romans 6:12–14

When you were slaves of sin, you were free from the control of righteousness. And what gain did that bring you? Things that now make you ashamed, for their end is death. But now, freed from the commands of sin and bound to the service of God, you have gains that lead to holiness, and the end is eternal life. For sin pays a wage, and the wage is death, but God gives freely, and his gift is eternal life in union with Christ Jesus our Lord.

Romans 6:20–23

I believe that to make real sense, to make sense in the real world, the Christian faith must be life-enhancing. It does not always, or often, feel like that. The magnificence of cathedrals, the sumptuousness of Christian art, the uplifting sound of Christian music, and messages full of eternal hope are completely at odds with dour religious practice that has traditionally concentrated on inherited guilt, sin, and moral failure. Whilst it may be virtuous to face up where we have gone wrong in our lives, to emphasise "sin" at the expense of all the good things that we are and can be stifles all our attempts at self-improvement. We need encouragement, support and understanding, not castigation, censure and rejection.

Paul's Letter to the Romans sets a tone that the church has always followed. Reject the sins of this world to enjoy a new life in the next. His message is designed to be helpful and hopeful, but his emphasis far from lifting our hopes throws us back on our failures as human beings. These failures, actual or potential, are far more real than the "salvation" he promises.

The church as the interpreter of the Bible message has always been the arbiter of right and wrong, but has not always practised what it preached. The numerous current and historic failures of the church to be an exemplar of its own message destroy its credibility, as does its inability to relate the blunt message of the New Testament to the complex ambiguities of daily life. If the avoidance of sin or moral failure requires an observance of a code that puts strictures around our lives and our behaviour, then it is no life at all. Seeking moral perfection in this way we destroy that essential part of us that is creative, loving and human.

I am not suggesting that the only way to get an excitement in life is to behave in a way that runs contrary to the Christian precepts which underpin the norms of behaviour in our society. I am looking for messages of hope that focus on the good that can happen here and now by adopting certain patterns of behaviour. I object to being told that the way forward is to "confess my sins" and vow to do better in future. None of us are perfect, and it would be a very boring and unsatisfactory world if we were. In our own way we all struggle to do what is right, and avoid what is wrong (though we may differ in how we define those two extremes). We do not need the modern equivalent of "fire and brimstone" preaching to help us on our moral way. Jean-Paul Sartre wrote that "hell is other people." They are indeed the hell we should worry about and believe in, not forgetting that is what we are to them.

We have all been brought up with the idea that "It is better to give than to receive." Repetition has made the phrase feel like religious motherhood and apple-pie. It takes many years of distance from childhood Christmases for it to mean anything, but now it does. Jesus was at pains to emphasise the overriding importance giving to and supporting others, no matter how marginalised and unsavoury. This was the way to put his teaching and preaching into action. The norms of social behaviour are irrelevant when we are faced with real need which we can help to alleviate. Our moral failure is that we do not do this.

I do not believe that we are all being asked to give huge sums to Children in Need, or to give a bed to someone homeless, or go out of our way to befriend a drug addict. The world is a better place because there are people who have the money, time, skills, and commitment to do just that. Most of us do not. I do not feel guilty at this kind of failure. I know my limitations, though I would be the first to admit that this may be an easy excuse for not making a bigger effort. I am sure that censure and criticism is more justified when we fail to do the less remarkable things that help us get on with each other. A word of thanks. A greeting. A helping hand. Willingness to listen. Sympathy and encouragement. It makes far more sense to me to explore the good that I can do, rather than wallow in a penitential pool full of all the things that I cannot do or have not done.

The passage from Jeremiah sums this up perfectly for me. We still talk about "prophets of doom." We are more than ready to believe that when bad things happens there is a supernatural reason for it. We always pay more attention to the bad news than the good, and we are far more aware of what is wrong with the world than what is right. An unremitting focus on our own failures is part of the same depressing habit. Jeremiah suggests that anyone can prophesy that bad things will happen and he will be believed because they usually do. Nothing has changed there. It takes a special kind of person to say with confidence that something good is going to happen, and he or she will not be recognised or believed until it does. Our responsibility is to believe that good things will happen, and make sure that they do.

Third Sunday after Trinity
Burdens of Guilt

Zechariah 9:9–12   Romans 7:15–25a
Psalm 145:8–15   Matthew 11:16–19, 25–30

The Lord is gracious and compassionate, long-suffering and ever faithful. The Lord is good to all; his compassion rests upon all his creatures.

Psalm 145:8–9

I know that nothing good dwells in me—my unspiritual self I mean—for though the will to do good is there, the ability to effect it is not. The good which I want to do, I fail to do; but what I do is the wrong which is against my will; and if what I do is against my will, clearly it is no longer I who am the agent, but sin that has its dwelling in me.

Romans 7:18–20

'Come to me, all you who are weary and whose load is heavy; I will give you rest. Take my yoke upon you, and learn from me, for I am gentle and humble-hearted; and you will find rest for your souls. For my yoke is easy to wear, my load is light.'

Matthew 11:28–30

WE ALL CARRY BAGGAGE. Suitcases of all shapes and sizes, stuffed with everything from failed relationships and gross behaviour to minor embarrassments and unintended slights. However much we would like to get rid of it, this baggage stays with us. The thoughts, memories, and emotions it carries creep up on us at unexpected moments, often in the small hours of the night. We relive the emotion and the shame, and the bag seems that much heavier. In the dark and deep places of our psyche, known only to us, time does not heal.

These burdens of guilt, whether small or large, have enormous power to depress our sense of our own worth and value. Our rational, daylight mind can unpack them, distance them, and if we are very brave encourage us to talk about them. This helps, but at times when we least expect them, we suddenly find we are carrying them again, and are dragged down by their weight.

Paul in his Letter to the Romans suggests that for him life is a more obvious battle between doing the right thing and doing the wrong thing. This is a matter of daily choice. Paul voices his deep sense of frustration, and guilt, that in his own life he continually fails to make the right choices. He recognises the course of action that he should take, but he cannot bring himself to follow it. Paul argues that this is because *sin has its dwelling in me.*

Paul's imagery is powerful, but for me, this personification of sin, is not helpful. Many people, then and now, would take this a step further, and say this is the Devil at work. I cannot use that kind of language. It may be irrational that I can entertain the concept of a spirit of good, but not a spirit of evil, but it does not fit in with my belief in the nature of creation.

The Psalmist and Matthew in the passages above offer us a picture of the nature of God that makes sense to me as a way in to understand how God works in us as a force for good. It is our ignorance or rejection of that which causes us to fail, make mistakes, upset other people, or simply behave in an unpleasant way. As a result the baggage gets heavier.

The characteristics that the Psalmist describes as belonging to God, are those that we would like to see in our fellow men and women. This is how we would like to be treated, and though we aspire to do the same, we frequently fail. The great difference between this image of God and ourselves, is that while we are frustrated by our collective failure to behave well, he is not. This for me the essence of divine encouragement.

The Psalms generally are for me not a very helpful or satisfying read. I enjoy some of the poetry, but I find the mixture of triumphalism, pastoral delight, breast-beating, and despair difficult to take. Psalm 145 however is a glorious hymn of praise to God that I find deeply affecting. The Psalmist's words shine a light on the gloom that arises from a concentration on "sin" in all its connotations.

We need the "grace" of God. This I interpret as a complex mixture of understanding and support, as part of his creation. We need compassion. For me that is concern for our failings and sympathy with our pain. We need long-suffering. That is not a word we use very much these days. Patience would be more common, but long-suffering feels more accurate. Over time that we cannot understand or compute God suffers because of and is patient with the failings of his creation which he hoped would be good but so often is not. We need faithfulness. A fair-weather friend is no friend at all. We need to be sure that however much we fail, however much we lack faith, however much we doubt, however much we argue about things that are unarguable, God will be there. Finally, we need to believe that the things that we need are common to the whole human race, and are offered to everyone in equal measure, so what right have we to discriminate.

Jesus, in Matthew's account, takes the personification of God one step further, in himself, and through his impact on us. It may seem that living life according to Christian principles is a burden because it simply adds to our sense of guilt and failure, but the opposite is true. By understanding the nature of God through Jesus we will find a more fulfilling way to live.

This is not a passive process. Jesus says *Take my yoke upon you, and learn from me.* We have to make a positive choice, not flirt with ideas, only putting them into practice when it suits us. The word *yoke* is common to all translations, and easily conjures up pictures of pain, weight, control, and submission, but Jesus makes it clear that his imagery is not designed to encouraged fear and subservience. His *yoke* reflects his character, which is *gentle and humble-hearted.* Like us, on a good day, and how we would like everyone to be. We need to make a positive choice to "learn." This for me is so much more effective that any absolute admonition to be this or do that. Learning is personal, thought-provoking, challenging, and life-changing. It can go to the heart of who we are and who we want to be. Jesus says that this is the way in which we will *find rest for our souls.* We can drop our own baggage for good.

Fourth Sunday after Trinity
Fruitful Seeds

Isaiah 55:10–13   Romans 8:1–11
Psalm 65   Matthew 13:1–9, 18–23

As the rain and snow come down from the heavens and do not return there without watering the earth, making it produce grain to give seed for sowing and bread to eat, so is it with my word issuing from my mouth; it will not return to me empty without accomplishing my purpose and succeeding in the task for which I sent it.

Isaiah 55:10–11

Those who live on the level of the old nature have their outlook formed by it, and that spells death; but those who live on the level of the spirit have the spiritual outlook and that is life and peace.

Romans 8:5–6

The seed sown among the thistles represents the person who hears the word, but worldly cares and the false glamour of wealth choke it, and it proves barren. But the seed sown on good soil is the person who hears the word and understands it; he does bear fruit and yields a hundredfold, or sixty fold, or thirtyfold.'

Matthew 13:22–23

THE PARABLE OF THE sower is a perceptive analysis of human behaviour. I have always read it as a description of the ways in which different types of people respond to new ideas and opportunities. Reading it again, I am struck for the first time by the realisation that it is not about how everyone else behaves, but how I behave. It sums up how I have responded to Christian teaching and the Christian faith over the years. It is not a sequential process, or a steady and positive development from the *footpath* to the *good soil*. To *bear fruit* most of the seed has to fall on good ground, but the same seed may fall in a variety of other places that are less fruitful. Each of us must find ways of achieving a positive balance, so that the harvest from the good soil is greater than that from anywhere else. This is not always easy.

The birds eat up the seed that falls on the footpath. Some ideas do not catch our imagination at all. They sit on the surface of our minds, superficially interesting, but we are quickly distracted by other things less challenging, more attractive, easier to assimilate, more in tune with our state of mind. The original ideas are then pushed to one side, or completely ignored. They had no intellectual or emotional roots, nothing in us helped them grow, so their superficial appeal was soon lost.

Some seed falls on rocky ground, but there is little soil. The seed sprouts quickly but is then destroyed by the sun. This is very familiar territory. A sudden enthusiasm that may seem all-consuming and life-changing, but quickly turns out to have no depth at all. When life becomes difficult or other distractions get in the way the enthusiasm dies. Other fads, other ideas, other movements shine brighter, and the first one fades to nothing. It is our own fickleness and lack of focus that results in failure.

I read Jesus' explanation of the *seed sown among thistles* as referring to the ideas which have great appeal but we do not have the mental and emotional strength to hold on to them. Our determination is not strong enough to withstand counter arguments or the appeal of an easier path in life. For some us it may well be literally the *false glamour of wealth* that leads us astray, but for most it will be anything that seems more appealing at the time, superficially attractive, without any depth of meaning, but none the less strong enough to ruin our best intentions.

The seed sown on good soil is of course the climax and the happy ending to this parable. The complex imagery suggests that I am both the soil in which the seed falls, and the sower in relation to the lives of other people, and the harvest that results from successful sowing. As Isaiah says in the passage above, the *word* is like rain that produces both *seed for sowing and bread to eat.* There is more here than just our understanding and acceptance. The harvest has to have a purpose. That purpose however is not the same for everyone.

I do not believe that Jesus' words listing the possible size of the harvest are a casual, throwaway remarks. He is saying that we will each of us respond in different ways to new ideas and moral challenges. For some there will be a radical change of life and a discovery of huge new opportunities that will eclipse anything they had experienced before. The rest of us may achieve more modest results, but this is not really a numbers game. The most important thing is that the seeds of new ideas do germinate in our lives and produce new ways of thinking and new ways of behaving.

Paul in his Letter to the Romans intellectualises so much that in the Gospels is clear because it is so simple. His great strength however is that he manages to compress difficult concepts into a few tightly chosen words. I find that reading this passage alongside the parable of the sower is helpful.

The footpath, the rocky ground, and the thistles represent for me distractions to understanding what Christian life really means. My personal distractions have taken various forms. I have tried to make sense of the Christian life while ignoring or rejecting the very things that make the Christian life what is, the teaching of Christ. I have devoted huge amounts of energy describing all the things that I do not like about Christian theology, behaviour, or church practice, and failed to think about what I do like. I have castigated priests for failing to preach in language that appeals to me, without giving any thought to what language that might be. This is my interpretation of living *on the level of the old nature.* Because it is all so negative, it inevitably leads to a kind of intellectual death, no good for me, no good for anyone else.

My *good soil* must be a *spiritual outlook* that accepts with good grace the things I may not yet understand, that recognises that I have a responsibility to try to understand, that sees my own dissatisfactions not as a selfish rebellion but a common cause with many, and above all wants to find a way to share ideas with others, so that we grow and bear mutual fruit.

Fifth Sunday after Trinity
Mixed Messages

Isaiah 44:6–8 Romans 8:12–25
Psalm 86:11–17 Matthew 13:24–30, 36–43

For all who are led by the Spirit of God are sons of God. The Spirit you have received is not a spirit of slavery, leading you back into a life of fear, but a Spirit of adoption, enabling us to cry 'Abba! Father!'

ROMANS 8:14–15

The Spirit of God affirms to our spirit that we are God's children; and if children, then heirs, heirs of God and fellow-heirs with Christ; but we must share his sufferings if we are also to share his glory.

ROMANS 8:16–17

'At the end of time the Son of Man will send his angels who will gather out of his kingdom every cause of sin, and all whose deeds are evil; these will be thrown into the blazing furnace, where there will be wailing and gnashing of teeth. Then the righteous will shine like the sun in the kingdom of their Father. If you have ears, then hear.'

MATTHEW 13:41–43

The Christian faith is not straightforward. Jesus' teaching was clear and unequivocal, yet he recognised that the vagaries of human nature made interpretation, and therefore life choices, difficult. Jesus' disciples and followers are on safe ground when they are retelling the story of his life, but their messages are mixed when they try to explain its meaning. The three passages above, two from Paul's letter to the Romans, and one from Matthew recording Jesus' words, highlight this problem.

Paul argues that belief in Jesus and a determination to follow his teaching gives us a new freedom to live life in a different way from ever before, in a new adoptive relationship with God that allows us to call him *Father* as Jesus himself did. This relationship is a very close one, epitomised by the use of the affectionate word *Abba*. This name sums up the special nature of the relationship as loving, intimate, nurturing, supportive, guiding, all the things you would expect of the best kind of parent. This is a good and safe place to be, but that is only part of the story.

Paul goes on to explain that being one of *God's children* carries with it a special responsibility. Paul uses the logic of genealogy to argue that our inheritance from God has as much to do with experiencing the same pain and suffering as Jesus here and now, as it has to do with sharing in the eternity of good things that will follow. Whilst we may look forward with hope, this teaching is pointing to an experience where *Abba, Father,* may feel as distant from us as he was for Jesus on the cross.

This raises a number of questions for us. What sort of parent, whether real or adoptive, offers both loving safety and pain and suffering in equal measure to their children? What form of measurement should we use to make sense of all this? Is this a version of tough love? Do we have to learn to grow up, accepting that this involves a certain amount of pain and emotional upset for every one of us? Is the way that we face the difficulties of life a living proof that we deserve the love that God has to offer? What difference will my "suffering", whatever form it takes, make to others? Is it not an odd belief that "suffering" here is a prerequisite of "glory" there? Am I expected to be a martyr to a cause that I do not fully understand for a mysterious reward that can only be found beyond time and space?

If all this seems contradictory and perplexing, the answer is usually to look at what Jesus said. In the passage from Matthew, his words are alarmingly clear, but they set up in my mind moral questions that add further layers of contradiction and mystery.

Jesus is preaching a fire and brimstone sermon, designed to strike fear into the hearts of his listeners. The moral extremes are clear. There is no middle ground. No questioning. No excuses. No extenuating circumstances. The bad go to a bad place and suffer, the good go to a good place and enjoy an even closer relationship with God. The message is simple and clear, in fact so simple and clear that Jesus' final admonition, *"If you have ears, then hear"* seems almost superfluous.

I do not believe he is simply telling his listeners to pay attention. That seems out of character. It makes much greater sense to interpret those words as meaning, "If you have heard what I have said, think deeply about what it means for you." In other words we are being asked to accept the truth of the two moral extremes he presents, but ask some taxing questions about what this means to us personally.

The end of time may well refer to what we usually call "the end of the world." We have no way of knowing whether this will be the ultimate cataclysm, whether man-made or natural, or a slow decay from a polluted atmosphere and pandemic disease. Our pessimistic expectations do not leave much room for angels or divine judgement.

On the other hand, for me, *the end of time* has a much more powerful meaning if it refers to our time, or my time here on earth. If I believe anything about a "final judgement", I believe it is here and now, in our lives. My understanding is that we all experience a continuous process of "judgement" through the consequences of our actions. When we come to the end of our life, to the end of our time, we will look back, and take stock, with pleasure we hope, with regret may be, or with grateful acceptance.

Jesus' words are a reminder that we need to need to think about all this now, not at the end of our time. Then it is too late.

Sixth Sunday after Trinity

Painful Images

1 Kings 3:5–12   Romans 8:26–39
Psalm 119:129–136   Matthew 13:31–33, 44–52

'Grant your servant, therefore, a heart with skill to listen, so that he may govern your people justly and distinguish good from evil. Otherwise who is equal to the task of governing this great people of yours?' The Lord was well pleased that this was what Solomon had asked for, and God said 'Because you have asked for this, and not for long life, or for wealth, or for the lives of your enemies, but have asked for discernment in administering justice, I grant your request.'

1 Kings 3:9–12

I am convinced that there is nothing in death or life, in the realms of spirits or superhuman powers, in the world as it is or the world as it shall be, in the forces of the universe, in heights or depths—nothing in all creation that can separate us from the love of God in Christ Jesus our Lord.

Romans 8:38–39

'The kingdom of Heaven is like a net cast into the sea, where it caught fish of every kind. When it was full, it was hauled ashore. Then the men sat down and collected the good fish into baskets, and threw the worthless away. That is how it will be at the end of time. The angels

> *will go out, and they will separate the wicked from the good and throw them into the blazing furnace, where there will be wailing and gnashing of teeth.'*
>
> MATTHEW 13:47–49

THERE ARE SEVEN REFERENCES to *wailing and gnashing of teeth* in the New Testament, two of them within ten verses of each other in Matthew chapter 13. The power of the image, and the repetition have ensured that the phrase has entered our own vocabulary as a vivid description of pain, frustration, and loss. That is for me as far as it goes. The suggestion that there will be some absolute, and irrevocable separation of the wicked from the good makes no sense to me.

This image of division, separation, and destruction does not sit happily with other passages which describe the nature of God and our relationship with him. It ignores the fact, of which Jesus must have been well aware, that there is good and evil in all of us. No one is completely good or completely evil, so the image runs contrary to our understanding of ourselves.

To use the images of fear, pain, and terror to drive home the opposite message is bad psychology. Jesus wants people to make a conscious choice to believe in him and live their lives in a new way. To do so because they are terrified of the consequences if they do not is not a sound basis for a fruitful and loving life. It is the kind of emotional slavery that is contrary to everything Jesus taught. I believe that fear of divine retribution is an absolute disincentive to profound belief.

It certainly works as a dramatic device to highlight the contrast between the life experience of those who believe in God and Jesus' teaching, and those who do not. The imagery is so convincing that we are drawn to the horror of it and so it gains a disturbing reality in our minds. It is however counter-productive.

There is a great deal of evidence for a different view that emphasises how life can be enriched and become more fulfilling. In the passages set for the Third Sunday after Trinity Jesus describes himself as *gentle and humble-hearted* and the Psalmist speaks of God as *gracious and compassionate, long-suffering and ever faithful*. In this Sunday's readings, Solomon is praised for asking for the *skill to listen* so that he can use *discernment in administering justice*. We can all recognise the importance of listening. With it comes the ability to understand both sides of any argument, and to understand the inner motivations and aspirations of other people. If we believe in a God who in human terms is the epitome of justice and understanding, it is impossible to accept simultaneously the idea of a God who meets out summary justice *at the end of time.*

Paul puts it even more powerfully in his Letter to the Romans: *Nothing in all creation can separate us from the love of God in Christ Jesus our Lord.* He is expressing an absolute belief in a loving God. There is no equivocation about who will be loved, or a ranking of the levels of "good" behaviour that will be required before we can receive that love. Jesus showed in his life that his love extended to everyone, particularly people on the margins of society who were ignored or rejected. He spent time with those whom others regarded as "sinners" or "worthless", so why did he preach pain and damnation for the "wicked"?

We cannot tell whether the Gospel accounts accurately reflect Jesus' own emphasis. Were these simply rhetorical devices to stir up his audience? Was he using dramatic language that would engage his listeners emotionally when he was describing something entirely mysterious and unknowable? Did he simply want to make people think differently, but found that his followers then and since took him literally? Probably all of those, and their effectiveness is proven by the fact that I am writing this now, trying to make sense of it all.

I believe that Jesus is talking about our lives now, not some apocalyptic vision of the end of the universe. That is not to say that the effects of living a less than virtuous life or behaving badly to other people are not equally devastating to us mentally. When we cause pain, consciously or unconsciously, and then regret it, our own pain and sense of failure is indeed an internal *wailing and gnashing of teeth.* We may well feel ashamed and alienated from other people as a result. We want to make amends, but it is often very difficult and painful to find a way back. We struggle to overcome our embarrassment and find words to convince others that we are not as bad as they think we are. This is a hellish experience, but there is a justice in the fact that we are suffering for the pain that we have caused. We are demeaned by it, and want to get out of the hole we have dug for ourselves. That is more than enough to encourage us make a conscious effort to try not to behave in that way again.

Seventh Sunday after Trinity
Enough Food

Isaiah 55:1–5   Romans 9:1–5
Psalm 145:8–9, 15–end Matthew 14:13–21

In all his promises the Lord keeps faith, he is unchanging in all his works; the Lord supports all who stumble and raises all who are bowed down. All raise their eyes to you in hope, and you give them their food when it is due. You open your hand and satisfy every living creature with your favour.

Psalm 145:14–16

The Lord is righteous in all his ways, faithful in all he does; the Lord is near to all who call to him, to all who call to him in sincerity. He fulfils the desire of those who fear him; he hears their cry and saves them. The Lord watches over all who love him, but the wicked he will utterly destroy.

Psalm 145:17–20

Then taking the five loaves and the two fish, he looked up to heaven, said the blessing, broke the loaves, and gave them to the disciples; and the disciples gave them to the people. They all ate and were satisfied; and twelve baskets were filled with what was left over. Some five thousand men shared in this meal, not counting women and children.

Matthew 14:18–21

Does belief in God make life better? This is not a question we often ask because most believers would argue that the answer must be "Yes." It is in the nature of God, as we understand it, to be so fully part of his creation that is impossible to question the meaning and value of his presence. He is it, and it is he.

Semantic pragmatists might argue that the only words we can use to describe God are the same we would use to describe the best of anything that we can imagine, an ultimate and quintessential state. By that definition the nature of God must be to be the best that can be.

Some would argue that God gives us answers to the ultimate questions about where we came from, why we are here, and where we are going. Without that knowledge we would live lives of doubt and uncertainty, so having that knowledge must make us happier and make sense of our lives.

The Psalmist offers us images of God as the omnipresent giver of life and support to all who believe in him. Who would not find their life enriched by a belief in a God who offers us, in some miraculous way, everything we want and need to live our lives to the full. The Psalmist, inevitably, argues that those who live evil lives and ignore the best that is implicit in God will find that their lives become steadily and inexorably worse, to the point that they lose everything good that makes life worth living.

The story of the feeding of the five thousand says the same thing. Some argue that the miracle lies not in any physical multiplication of a small number of loaves and fishes, but in the fact that Jesus inspired people to share what they already had with each other. This is an attractive idea, but not one that has much appeal for me. It seems too simplistic and I wonder why Jesus did not make the meaning more obvious. I think the meaning goes deeper than that.

We need food to sustain life. Jesus talks often about "spiritual food" and he likens himself to water, bread, and wine. Our belief in him sustains our spiritual lives. This to my mind lies at the heart of the story of the loaves and fishes. We are told that faced with the demands of a huge crowd, who want to hear what he has to say, Jesus' *heart went out to them*. He tells the disciples to *"give them something to eat yourselves"* but they complain that they only have the five loaves and two fish. The disciples, as so often before, respond to the literal meaning of what Jesus says, without realising what he is asking them to do.

Jesus prays for inspiration, and then begins preaching, and his disciples move among the crowd, talking and helping people to understand what is being said. The multiplication of the loaves and fishes is simply a way of describing the impact of his words on this huge crowd, and the part the disciples play in supporting and counselling people who heard what Jesus had to say. If God is the giver of spiritual life and support to all who believe in him, then his son must emulate him, as he does in this story.

It is important, I believe, to respond to both parts of the story. Everybody in the crowd *ate and were satisfied; and twelve baskets were filled with what was left over.* The surplus is as important as the initial distribution. People were more than satisfied with what they heard, and would have had difficulty absorbing more at that time. Not only was Jesus offering food for thought then, but ideas and concepts that could sustain people long after.

The surplus represents the fact that Jesus' teaching always goes further than we might expect, both in meaning and in the number of people it affects. The twelve baskets clearly refer back to the disciples. Their experience with this crowd was an early test of their ministry. They would later extend their ministry far and wide, a living proof of the impact of Jesus' life and teaching. The final count of *five thousand men*, plus, as we might say, their families, simply emphasises how extensive and successful this outreach was.

The crowd clearly felt better, and that is how we should feel. The Psalmist captures the mood perfectly using words which the story of the feeding of the five thousand is a living example from Jesus' life: *You open your hand and satisfy every living creature with your favour.*

Our belief in God, and our understanding of him, which are different for each and every one of us, are a continual source of spiritual and intellectual food. We have to choose how much we can take at any one time, and how much we can share with others. There is always more than enough, and more than we will ever need.

Eighth Sunday after Trinity

Storms of Faith

1 Kings 19:9–18   Romans 10:5–15
Psalm 65:8–13   Matthew 14:22–33

The Lord was passing by: a great strong wind came, rending mountains and shattering rocks before him, but the Lord was not in the wind; and after the wind there was an earthquake, but the Lord was not in the earthquake; and after the earthquake fire, but the Lord was not in the fire; and after the fire a faint murmuring sound. When Elijah heard it he wrapped his face in his cloak and went out and stood at the entrance to the cave.

I Kings 19:11–13

He made the disciples embark and cross to the other side ahead of him, while dismissed the crowd; then he went up the hill by himself to pray. It had grown late, and he was there alone. The boat was already some distance from the shore, battling with a head wind and rough sea. Between three and six in the morning he came towards them, walking across the lake.

Matthew 14:22–25

Peter got down out of the boat, and walked over the water towards Jesus. But when he saw the strength of the gale he was afraid, and beginning to sink, he cried, 'Save me Lord!' Jesus at once reached out and caught hold of him. 'Why did you hesitate?' he said. 'How little faith you have!'

Matthew 14:29–31

STORMS OF FAITH

AFTER FEEDING THE FIVE thousand Jesus wanted to be alone to pray. This for me is further evidence that he had just gone through a huge, and emotionally draining experience. His empathy with the huge crowd, who had followed him, we are told, *to a remote place*, and his success in engaging their attention had sapped his energy. He needed time by himself to unwind and restock his spiritual batteries. Even in his world, however, things did not always go according to plan.

There are many references throughout the Bible to God's power over and his presence in extreme weather. A sudden storm at this particular moment can be interpreted as a response to Jesus' prayers, but not a response he was expecting. Far from being given time for restorative meditation Jesus is being reminded that he still has work to do. That work has to start closer to home than he might have expected. The disciples who had served him well with the huge crowds, are now in difficulty, and they need his help.

It does not matter whether or how Jesus "walked on water", the image is powerful enough without further analysis. In their hour of great need Jesus appeared to the disciples, showing that he was not affected by high winds and rough seas. Not surprisingly they had difficulty believing that is was him, a situation that would reoccur in future. They were terrified, he was calm, and that calm gave them new confidence.

The echoes of Elijah's experience in 1 Kings give even greater depth to the story. Elijah expected God's presence to be found in huge winds, earthquakes and fire as they reflected his understanding of who God was and what he could do. The truth was very different. The power lies not in extraordinary external events, but what we hear internally, here described as *a faint murmuring sound*, or in other translations *a still small voice*. When Elijah hears this he realises that God is with him.

In the middle of a huge storm, Jesus appears to the disciples and calms their fears with a few quiet words, *"Take heart. It is I. Do not be afraid."* Jesus has helped his disciples overcome their immediate external problem, but it is soon clear that there is a more insidious problem to be addressed.

Peter wants to emulate Jesus, and prove himself, by also walking on the water. Jesus encourages him to do so, but then Peter's bravado fails and he begins to sink. Jesus saves him, but chastises him for his hesitation and lack of faith. Jesus must have felt, not for the first or the last time, that it was going to be an uphill struggle preparing his disciples for their future role, if Peter's behaviour was an example of their personal confidence and faith.

Jesus and Peter climb into the boat and the wind drops. There is no suggestion in Matthew's account that Jesus caused the wind to drop, but the disciples clearly believed that he did. In the space of a few minutes they have experienced Jesus appearing in the middle of a storm, apparently walking on water, Peter trying to do the same and failing, Jesus saving him from drowning, and the storm dying down. No wonder that *the men in the boat fell at his feet, exclaiming, "You must be the Son of God."* Jesus could not have asked for better evidence that they were ready to carry his message forward. His prayers have been answered.

In Matthew's Gospel the story of the feeding of the five thousand and the storm is told in just thirty verses. It is worth exploring the story at some length because it says a great deal to me, through hints and references to themes of enormous power and resonance. The impact of Christ's teaching as sustaining food for thought. The disciple's developing role as ministers. Misconceptions about how we experience God's presence with us. Fear and trust. The need for confidence in the face of extreme situations. The quietness that is the reality of our spiritual understanding, against the noise of external events and influences. Our understanding of what we believe our faith requires and expects of us. The realisation that after all the storm and stress of our daily lives there is something in all this that we may not understand but which commands our attention and respect.

That puts me, and I suspect many others, in the same position as Peter on the boat. He was willing to accept the reality of something that he could not understand intellectually. He was inspired to follow an extraordinary example. He wanted to show his mentor and friend that he was a worthy follower. Against all his natural inclinations he stepped off the boat, and then the brutal reality of his decision hit him. He sank. How often does my initial enthusiasm and excitement come to nothing because I am distracted, I think too much, I over analyse, I begin to doubt my own feelings, and I sink? I do not have enough faith to believe anyone will catch hold of me.

Ninth Sunday after Trinity

Crumbs of Learning

Isaiah 56:1, 6–8   Romans 11:1–2a, 29–32
Psalm 67   Matthew 15:10–28

May God be gracious to us and bless us, may he cause his face to shine on us, that your purpose may be known on earth, and your saving power among all nations.

Psalm 67:1–2

A Canaanite woman from those parts came to meet him crying, "Son of David! Have pity on me; my daughter is tormented by the devil." But he said not a word in reply. His disciples came and urged him: "Send her away! See how she comes shouting after us." Jesus replied, "I was sent to the lost sheep of the house of Israel, and to them alone."

Matthew 15:22–24

The woman came and fell at his feet and cried, "Help me, sir." Jesus replied, 'It is not right to take the children's bread and throw it to the dogs.' 'True, sir,' she answered, 'and yet the dogs eat the scraps that fall from the master's table.' Hearing this Jesus replied, 'What faith you have! Let it be as you wish!' And from that moment her daughter was restored to health.

Matthew 15:25–28

READINGS FROM THE GOSPELS are surrounded by so much liturgical reverence that their astonishing modernity is obscured. In the story from Matthew we have a distraught woman who has a daughter with mental health problems. Jesus gives her the cold shoulder, followed more vocally by the disciples who want to get rid of her. Jesus then justifies his and their behaviour by arguing that his mission is only to the Jews, yet his whole life and teaching contradicts that. The woman is persistent, and Jesus now chooses to respond with a challenging yet enigmatic comment. She replies with such aplomb, that Jesus sees her in an entirely different light, commends her faith, and cures her daughter. What is going on?

Matthew's account may be truncated so that the sequence of events is difficult to follow. There is a clearer and more coherent version in Mark chapter 7. Matthew may also be guilty of putting words into Jesus' mouth that reflect his faulty understanding of Jesus' mission. All of that is easy to explain. Jesus' enigmatic words are not. This for me is the heart of the story, and deserves further exploration.

Jesus uses simple words to talk about profound truths. This strategy guarantees easy acceptance of what he says, memory that lasts the test of time (as the Gospel accounts demonstrate), and that nagging feeling that simple as they are, these words need further thought. He is also adept at using images that are familiar both as being part of everyday life and as metaphors for deeper ideas that he has talked about on other occasions.

There is no doubt in my mind that in the crowds following Jesus there were people calling for his help with some personal crisis whenever he appeared. Some of these were doubtless sincere, some chancers seeking the limelight, some with problems of their own. To be continually battered by calls for help must have been exhausting. Jesus must have felt this more than most. Not only because he was the object of their attention, but because he could not physically help everyone, and not everyone deserved his help.

It is uncomfortable to us to think that Jesus discriminated in any way, but I believe that he was trying to explain to his followers that it was important to separate the genuine from the false. Trying to help everyone, irrespective of their level of need or motivation is not a good strategy for any philanthropic mission.

Jesus had said: *Let the children come to me; do not try to stop them; for the kingdom of God belongs to such as these* (Luke 18:16). We need to cultivate childlike qualities of innocent enquiry, exploration and discovery, growing understanding, and honest and open response, if we are to truly appreciate what he is saying. Our normal adult responses frequently lack these characteristics. We equivocate, challenge, over-intellectualise, analyse to death, second guess, and decide that we know better, if not best.

Jesus's purpose is to help us understand our spiritual nature, discover new ways of looking at the world, and encourage behaviour that is life-affirming. All this needs careful nurturing and support. Not everyone responds to this in the same way. For some it is nonsense, others question and challenge, others accept fully. Jesus wants his teaching to spread as quickly as possible, and though his perspective may be eternal, he needs early success, and that will come from choosing people who are, in modern parlance, "early adopters." There is no point in offering new ideas and teaching to people who are unlikely to be responsive or supportive. The uninterested or the unsuccessful are the worst ambassadors.

This is the practical logic of modern marketing, yet in human terms it is deeply flawed. Jesus must have known that his own mission and life itself was more complex, as does the women to whom he was talking. His purpose was indeed to "save the world", a phrase that we use so loosely now that its impact has been irretrievably diluted. The psalmist captured it well in his prayer that *your purpose may be known on earth, and your saving power to all nations.*

The woman pointed out that however hard you try to limit any message to a few, others will hear it and respond, in their own way, in their own time, at their own pace. She recognised Jesus' wider purpose. He recognised that she had a vision that went far beyond her present circumstances. He commended the breadth and depth of her faith, and responded to her request.

The scraps under the table can be understood alongside the surplus after the feeding of the five thousand. Jesus' teaching is such that even crumbs can make a difference. Cranmer, in what we now call the Prayer of Humble Access said "We not worthy to gather up the crumbs under thy table." I believe we are, and Jesus is saying that whoever we are we can.

Tenth Sunday after Trinity
Skills and Belief

Isaiah 51:1–6   Romans 12:1–8
Psalm 138   Matthew 16:13–20

'Let us use the different gifts allotted to us by God's grace: the gift of inspired utterance, for example, let us use in proportion to our faith; the gifts of administration to administer, the gift of teaching to teach, the gift of counselling to counsel.

ROMANS 12:6–7

If you give to charity, give without grudging; if you are a leader, lead with enthusiasm; if you help others in distress, do it cheerfully.

ROMANS 12:8

'And you,' he asked, 'who do you say I am?' Simon Peter answered: 'You are the Messiah, the Son of the living God.' Then Jesus said: 'Simon son of Jonah, you are favoured indeed! You did not learn that from any human being: it was revealed to you by my heavenly Father. And I say to you: you are Peter, the Rock; and on this rock I will build my church, and the powers of death shall never conquer it.'

MATTHEW 16:15–18

THE LIST OF GIFTS in Paul's letter to the Romans is more down to earth than the list in the First Letter to the Corinthians (see Day of Pentecost/Whit Sunday), but it is clear that he is selecting examples of the gifts that he considered particularly important. They cover an interesting range which is as relevant today as it was in the first century after Jesus' birth.

The first gift is *inspired utterance* which is more understandable than the more common translation *prophecy*. Paul adds an important caveat that we should use this gift *in proportion to our faith*. This has many implications. He is telling us that we should not get carried away in what we say or preach. We should talk about what we know and believe, because that will make what we say convincing and inspiring. There is no place for rousing rhetoric whose purpose is purely theatrical if this is not based on personal and unwavering conviction. Put simply, we have to believe what we say.

The gift of administration may seem rather prosaic, but Paul recognises that it is an essential gift if we want to get anything done. Faith, conviction, emotional integrity, inspired preaching are not in themselves enough. We have to be able to bring people together, organise meetings, find out who can do what, and delegate jobs. Our purpose may be spiritual but it must be supported by the mundane systems that make any organization work effectively.

Teaching and *counselling* are an interesting pairing. These two gifts highlight the fact that to get our message across we have to understand the different ways people learn, and the kind of support that they need. "Coaching" and "mentoring" would be a modern equivalent.

We all need the skills of a teacher to put information across, help others' understanding, and encourage their own learning, but this is only part of the story. We all have hang-ups and prejudices about what we are told. We do not want to be taught. We think we know it all. We need help to understand what we do not know, and what we need to know. This can happen if someone sits with us to advise sympathetically and draw out our own understanding of our needs.

Paul then changes his theme from the gifts that we need to the way we behave because it is behaviour that will guarantee that we use the skills that we have effectively.

Today charitable fund-raising is an industry, and we all suffer from charity fatigue. Not a night goes by without television advertisements designed to pluck at our heart strings encouraging donations of "just" £2 or £5 a month to cure cancer, stop child abuse, save donkeys, look after dogs, support lifeboats, protect wildlife, or help older people. The list goes on and on. We recognise the need but begrudge the pressure. Paul's advice that if we give to charity we should *give without grudging* is particularly apposite today. Hard as it may seem, genuine giving must be sincere and wholehearted. We must not give under pressure or from a sense of obligation or because it is a good thing to be seen to be doing. It must be a matter of belief in both the act of giving and the purpose of the gift.

Finally Paul gives two pieces of advice that go to the heart of how to be effective leaders and helpers. We need enthusiasm and cheerfulness. Leaders need enthusiasm because enthusiasm is infectious. It encourages others to be as passionate about a cause or a project or an organisation as the leader is. Helpers need to be cheerful because this also is infectious. Cheerfulness shows that the help is gladly given. No one wants to be feel that it is a burden. If we are down, we want someone cheerful to help us up, anything else will simply make a bad situation worse.

If we put together the gifts that Paul lists in his letters to the Romans and the Corinthians, we have a remarkable blueprint for any priest, minister or leader. He or she needs the ability to preach well and explain difficult ideas, finding the right words for their audience, and always basing what they say on their own belief. They need interpersonal skills that will heal rifts and emotional distress and the ability to judge others' sincerity and inner motivations. They need to be teachers and counsellors, open-hearted givers, enthusiastic leaders, and cheerful helpers.

When Jesus selected Peter as *the rock* on which he would build his church, he did not prepare a job description and interview Peter to find out whether his skills matched those that were required. He asked one question about Peter's belief: *"Who do you say that I am?"* Peter answered with absolute conviction though he had no empirical evidence to support his answer. He believed that Jesus was the Son of God, and from that belief everything else flowed and grew.

It is always tempting to believe that logical analysis of our skills will show us what we should do with them. What I am therefore determines what I can be. Jesus tells us that before that I need to decide what I believe, because what I believe makes me what I am.

Eleventh Sunday after Trinity

Harsh Words

Jeremiah: 15:15–21   Romans 12:9–end
Psalm 26:1–8   Matthew 16:21–end

Live in agreement with one another. Do not be proud, but be ready to mix with humble people. Do not keep thinking how wise you are. Never pay back evil for evil. Let your aims be such as all count honourable. If possible, as far as it lies with you, live at peace with all.

Romans 12:16–18

From that time Jesus began to make it clear to his disciples that he had to go to Jerusalem, and endure great suffering at the hands of the elders, chief priests, and scribes; to be put to death, and to be raised again on the third day. At this Peter took hold of him and began to rebuke him: 'Heaven forbid!' he said. 'No, Lord, this shall never happen to you.' Then Jesus turned and said to Peter, 'Out of my sight, Satan; you are a stumbling block to me. You think as men think, not as God thinks.'

Matthew 16:21–23

Jesus then said to his disciples, 'Anyone who wishes to be a follower of mine must renounce self; he must take up his cross and follow me. Whoever wants to save his life will lose it, but whoever loses his life for my sake will find it.'

Matthew 16:24–25

Jesus had called Peter *'the rock on which I will build my church'*. Peter clearly had an impetuous nature and tended to speak his mind. This aggressive determination was a characteristic that Jesus recognised as vital if the Christian community was to grow and spread. There was no place for soft-touch piety and easy platitudes. Painful things had to be said, difficult things done, and hard experiences endured, a continuous re-enactment of Jesus' own life. Peter was his own worst enemy and Jesus recognised that he needed to be carefully managed, and at times held in check.

Jesus had been fairly reticent about the end of his life. He did not want to depress his disciples or distract them from the work that he and they were still doing. The time came, however, when he had to begin to prepare them for the worst and the best that was to come. Peter, though blessed with insights into Jesus' real nature, was not prepared for or ready to accept this shocking announcement. He wanted to stop it happening because he could not bear the thought of losing the man he loved and respected above all others. He did not understand the real meaning of the *Messiah* that he has so confidently claimed Jesus was. Jesus was understandably frustrated at this lack of perception.

Jesus' early confidence that Peter was *favoured indeed* because his understanding of Jesus' nature was divinely inspired was dented. Peter's understanding was limited. He said the right words, but did not really understand their meaning. Peter is us.

Jesus rounded on Peter, as he had done to other disciples many times before when they failed to really understand what he was saying. This was a time leading up to the most important, unavoidable and horrific events of Jesus' life. In his own mind he had difficulty accepting what he had to face, so it was a natural human reaction to turn on those who voiced his own fears. The last thing any of us want, when we are facing pain or distress, is a well-meaning friend reminding us of our own fears. Jesus knew that Peter's response was deeply ingrained in his character. He needed a sharp response to make him realise what he had done. We are taken aback by the force of Jesus' words which are a wake-up call to us all. At moments of great stress, when our heartfelt emotions dominate all our rational thoughts, Jesus is demanding that we think differently. But how do any of us think *as God thinks*?

Jesus was asking Peter to try to understand God's wider purpose, and it seems to me that in whatever way we can, that is what we need to do. From one perspective, our life is a speck in time, so small as to seem irrelevant, in the grand scheme of things. That phrase itself acknowledges that we are part of something bigger than we can ever imagine. The fact there is much beyond and around us that we do not understand does not invalidate the importance of our part in it. We have a purpose here, even if we cannot articulate what that is.

Jesus' explanation to the disciples after his outburst to Peter takes this a step further. The disciples must have been shocked by Jesus' reaction, particularly after his confidence in Peter as the foundation of his church. Their own thoughts must have echoed Peter's, so they must have felt the rebuke personally. He tells them that they must be prepared to put their own feelings and reactions to one side if they are going to follow him in all senses of that word. Hanging on to what they know and trust will not get them very far because in a new world order new thinking and new behaviour are required. Life will never be the same again. They will lose all the certainties that they thought they had, but in this new life they will discover new purpose and new meaning.

Our purpose here will have much, if not everything, to do with the way we behave with and respond to other people. We will have a miserable life if we alienate everyone, and Paul in his Letter to the Romans gives us six simple guidelines to ensure that does not happen. We need to try to get on with people; avoid arrogance or superiority; not take revenge if any harm is done to us; lead an honest life that others can admire. He sums it up with a wish that we should *live in peace with all,* but he recognises the foibles and frailties of our human nature in the caveats *If possible* and *as far as it lies with you.* It is not always as straightforward as it sounds. Knowing what is right is not always a guarantee that we will do what is right, and there are always other people to blame.

There will always be moments when our emotions get the better of us. Our frustrations and prejudices show. We hurt other people and we hurt ourselves. We behave in ways that we regret afterwards. In the moment we take the short view. Hindsight always gives us the long view. If we believe that God is beyond time in his eyes we are more than a moment or a speck. To think as God thinks is to have a view of our lives that embraces the moment, however painful, as having meaning. When we try to work out what the new purpose of our lives might be, our challenge is to work out what that meaning is.

Twelfth Sunday after Trinity
Love and Orgies

Ezekiel 33:7–11   Romans 13:8–end
Psalm 119:33–40   Matthew 18:15–20

The commandments, 'You shall not commit adultery, you shall not commit murder, you shall not steal, you shall not covet' and any other commandment there may be, are all summed up in one rule, 'Love your neighbor as yourself.'

ROMANS 13:9–10

Always remember that this is the hour of crisis; it is high time for you to wake out of sleep, for deliverance is nearer to us now than it was when we first believed. It is far on in the night; day is near. Let us therefore throw off the deeds of darkness and put on the armour of light. Let us behave with decency as befits the day: no drunken orgies, no debauchery or vice, no quarrels or jealousies! Let Christ Jesus himself be the armour that you wear; give your unspiritual nature no opportunity to satisfy its desires.

ROMANS 13:11–14

'Where two or three meet together in my name, I am there among them.'

MATTHEW 18:20

LOVE AND ORGIES

WHEN WE THINK ABOUT how to live our lives, is our mind-set influenced most by the Ten Commandments or the Sermon on the Mount? Is it easier to be told what we must not do, or to be advised what we should do? Do we find it as difficult to accept one as it is the other? Do we want a life without the burden of moral strictures, while accepting that we are not advocating moral license? Is *loving your neighbor as yourself* the easy option, or the most difficult option of all? These are the questions that the verses from Paul's letter to the Romans raise in my mind. I find them disconcerting.

Five of the Ten Commandments are about belief in God, and one is about the importance of parents and family. The last five are the prohibitions listed by Paul. These are still largely the moral basis on which we live, so much so that we accept them as a given, though adultery and coveting may now lack some of their original force. Paul realised that and wanted to promote Jesus' more positive rule that would encourage people to commit to a new way of life. This was what we now call the "golden rule", loving your neighbor as yourself, or doing as you would be done by. This makes absolute sense to me, but not everyone sees the world in that way. Loving your (difficult, obstreperous, selfish, opinionated, aggressive, rude) neighbor or colleague is not easy. We all need to find coping mechanisms long before we describe our behaviour as demonstrating love.

Paul was less subtle than Jesus, and is something of the moral martinet in his letters, and doubtless his preaching. He felt the need to tell people what they must not do. He does so in some complex imagery of day and night. Day is light of the Second Coming and a new world order. Night represents the current state of the world. His list of what is wrong is on a sliding scale from the drunken orgies that may be enjoyed by a few to the quarrels and jealousy of which we are all guilty. He argues that we need to focus on spiritual things to avoid the temptations that are around us, with Jesus' example and teaching as our defense. That is too much pious exhortation for me to take.

I can live with imagery in which darkness and light represent the 'bad' and 'good' side of my personality, but the idea of a Second Coming does not help me in any way. I am left wondering do I, or any of us, need to be told what not to do? Do we not know that already? We will make our own choices. These choices may or may not include Paul's *drunken orgies, debauchery and vice*, but they will almost certainly include *quarrels* and petty *jealousies*. So where is the value of biblical exhortations that are morally right, yet seem out of touch with where and who we are?

This emphasis on what we must not do gives Christianity the dour and forbidding image commonly associated with former times and practices. People are straitlaced and so nervous about the bad things that might happen to them that they have no time to take pleasure in the good things of life that are there for all to enjoy. I do not believe that Jesus wanted this. Over time there has been a wholesale betrayal of his message that was all about a new way of living. I believe he wanted us to live to the full and realise our potential. A destructive agenda of extreme moral rectitude fails absolutely to do that. Sadly it is easier to preach "you shall not" than it is to preach *love your neighbor as yourself.*

The last two words, *as yourself,* carry as much weight and importance as the first three. We can spend hours debating the nature of love in circumstances where we are faced with those who in our eyes are unlovable. We can admire the example of those who have managed to do that in situations that are far more extreme than any we are likely to experience. Admiration, however, does not always encourage emulation. We tell ourselves that we do not have, by nature, the gifts of empathy and selflessness that others seem to possess. This is just an excuse. Our failure is not knowing ourselves well enough really to understand what we want from others and what we can give to them. Loving them may not be as a big a deal as we first thought.

We are taught, though we may not understand, that Jesus' life and death were an expression of God's love for us. We are taught also that we are by nature unlovable and unworthy of this, though we may not believe that. We are also taught that God is always with us, no matter who we are or what we do. That for me is the positive side of all pulpit pessimism about our "sinful nature."

I would like to think that *Where two or three meet together in my name, I am there among them* is less about prayer-meetings and church services (because why should they have preferential treatment) and more about how we live with each other. Jesus is saying that he is there in our attempts to love our neighbors, against the odds, as ourselves, because he is in us and part of those faltering attempts at love. That is the reason why our small efforts can have unexpected results that make life worth living.

Thirteenth Sunday after Trinity
Forgiving Ourselves

Genesis 50:15–21 Romans 14:1–12
Psalm 103:1–13 Matthew 18:21–35

The Lord is compassionate and gracious, long-suffering and ever faithful; he will not accuse or nurse his anger for ever. He has not treated us as our sins deserve or repaid us according to our misdeeds. As the heavens tower high above the earth, so outstanding is his love towards those who fear him. As far as east is from west, so far from us has he put away our offences. As a father has compassion on his children, so the Lord has compassion on those who fear him; for he knows how we were made, he remembers that we are but dust.

Psalm 103: 8–14

Then Peter came to him and asked, 'Lord how often am I to forgive my brother if he goes on wronging me? As many as seven times?' Jesus replied, 'I do not say seven times but seventy times seven.'

Matthew 18:21–22

'"You scoundrel! I cancelled the whole of your debt when you appealed to me; ought you not to have shown mercy to your fellow-servant just as I showed mercy to you?" And so angry was the master that he condemned the man to be tortured until he should pay the debt in full. That is how my heavenly Father will deal with you, unless you each forgive your brother from your hearts.'

Matthew 18:32–35

FORGIVENESS IS NOT A numbers game. Peter's suggestion that he should forgive seven times would have seemed extravagant as it was more than double Jewish teaching at that time. Jesus rejects and ridicules this with an even more extravagant number. I do not believe he meant this to be taken literally in any measurable, mathematical sense. It was simply a huge number that was beyond counting. Some people have argued that the meaning of the numbers is connected to lifetimes of seventy years. This is an attractive idea, not in terms of the numbers, but the expectation. We are expected to go on forgiving others throughout our lives, for ever. There is no counting involved. This is something we have to do.

I would like to think that in the word *brother* there is a more subtle and personal message. There is no doubt that *my bother* can mean anyone, family, friend, colleague, acquaintance, or someone completely unknown to me with whom I come into contact. In that sense, I have to forgive everybody, no matter who they are or what they have done to me.

My feeling is that Peter's question has just as much to do with how we forgive those who are closest to us. The hurt and unhappiness that can be caused within families is often the most difficult to heal. Complex emotions are involved when those we love or who are supposed to love us behave in a way that betrays that trust and belief. The pain is intense, the anger deep-seated, and the sense of rejection profound. In such circumstances forgiveness is not easy. In such circumstances forgiveness is the only way to move on.

The concept of forgiveness is complicated by apparently mixed Biblical messages. In Psalm 103, the Psalmist repeats the four characteristics of God, *compassionate and gracious, long-suffering and ever faithful.* His compassion is infinite, he has completely negated the importance of our various failures, and he cares for us even though we are insignificant creatures. Jesus echoes this in his advice to Peter on life-long forgiveness, but he then tells a story that suggests that God will be anything but compassionate and caring to those who fail to forgive as they have been forgiven. Lack of forgiveness is punished by no forgiveness at all. On the surface this seems to be a contradiction not a confirmation.

The story, for dramatic effect, puts great emphasis on the servant being thrown into prison and tortured for what he has done. The meaning lies deeper and is more personal. My failure to forgive will mean that I will suffer mental torture, anxiety, and unhappiness until I do. The story suggests that this is something that God does to me as a punishment. In real life this is something that I bring on myself. My behaviour will cause me pain and suffering until I put things right and 'forgive my brother from my heart'.

All this is very easy to say, but very difficult to do. I can easily make a list of all the things people have done to me over time that I resent or feel a grievance about. In many of these cases time has not healed at all, but made things worse. I am already torturing myself. In quiet moments of reflection I know that this is no way to live. I must put these things out of my mind as they no longer have any consequence or meaning in my life. This may be some way from any tangible act of forgiveness, but it comes to the same thing. Do I have enough self-awareness to turn hurt and resentment into acceptance and forgetting?

I certainly have a continuous mental list, when I care to call it to mind, of things done to me that I resent. The opposite though is not true. I do not spend time on thinking about things I have done to other people which deserve their forgiveness. I mentally blank out moments of embarrassment when I have caused pain or distress, consciously or unconsciously. We all think that we are better people than we really are, and are frequently taken by surprise by other peoples' opinions that contradict our own benevolent view of ourselves. I am therefore not predisposed to think badly of myself if I can possibly help it. I am disposed to nurse and nurture the resentment I feel about the behaviour of other people towards me. What makes me better than them?

To forgive others is a two-way process that involves a heart-felt understanding of the nature of any hurt received that requires forgiveness and of any hurt given that requires understanding. It is only when we recognise why we feel pain and resentment at the behaviour of others that we can begin to relate that to the way we behave ourselves. We need to be sensitive to why and how people have hurt us so that we can recognise in ourselves the ability to do the same to others. The closer to home that forgiveness is required the more difficult it is. The act of forgiveness that requires the most effort is that which we offer to ourselves. That is the only way we can begin to understand what forgiving others really means.

Fourteenth Sunday after Trinity
Personal Worth

Jonah 3:10–4:end   Philippians 1:21–end
Psalm 145:1–8   Matthew 20:1–16

'The kingdom of Heaven is like this. There was once a landowner who went out early one morning to hire labourers for his vineyard; and after agreeing to pay them the usual day's wage he sent them off to work. Three hours later he went out again and saw some more men standing idle in the marketplace. "Go and join the others in the vineyard," he said, "and I will pay you a fair wage," and off they went.'

MATTHEW 20:1–4

'When the evening fell the owner of the vineyard said to the overseer, "Call the labourers and give them their pay, beginning with those who came last, and ending with the first." Those who had started work an hour before sunset came forward and were paid the full day's wage. When it was the turn of the men who had come first, they expected something extra, but were paid the same as the others.'

MATTHEW 20:8–10

'As they took it, they grumbled at their employer: "These latecomers did only one hour's work, yet you have treated them on a level with us, who have sweated the whole day long in the blazing sun!" The owner turned to one of them and said, "My friend, I am not being unfair

> *to you. You agreed on the usual wage for the day, did you not? Take your pay and go home. I choose to give the last man the same as you. Surely I am free to do what I like with my own money? Why be jealous because I am generous?" So the last will be first, and the first last.'*

MATTHEW 20:11–16

It may well be heretical to suggest that the parable of the labourers in the vineyard is not the most successful of Jesus' parables, but I am tempted to think that may be one of the reasons why it appears only in Matthew's Gospel. Did other Gospel writers find it difficult to understand, or did its obscurity lead to some failure in transmission from person to person. Images and stories used as metaphors for the most profound ideas are powerful aids to understanding if the ideas take us to somewhere new and hitherto not thought of. They work less well if we become so bogged down in the intricacies of the story that we miss the bigger picture. I think there is a tendency for this to happen with this story. It contains so many themes and sub-themes that it is easy to be tempted down byways of interpretation that obscure its immediate message. The first sentence is all important. Jesus is putting into accessible language the difficult concept of *the kingdom of Heaven*, yet the simplicity of the language and the story invite human parallels that are less than helpful.

I believe that the *kingdom of Heaven* is a way of describing the world of the spirit in each and every one of us. Our understanding of God comes through our understanding of our inner selves. The *kingdom of Heaven* is therefore not somewhere to go but something to be. By understanding our role and purpose here we will come to have some small, infinitesimal understanding of God's own purpose. His purpose is by definition beyond our understanding because it is beyond our concepts of time and space. The *kingdom of Heaven* therefore is something in us that has the attributes of God that cannot be defined in human terms. How then do we make sense of this parable?

If the landowner is God, who are we? Is the vineyard our life, or the world as a whole? Is being "hired" a metaphor for belief or service or both? Are we "hired" to make sense of our lives or to contribute to productive growth in the world as a whole? In relation to our life, have we been hired yet? Is "idleness" a lack of commitment, a lack of curiosity, a reluctance to accept guidance, or simply intellectual and emotional laziness? Is "idleness" a negative choice or a positive opportunity? Is the working day our life or the whole of history? Does the "hour" of our calling matter? Who are the "latecomers", the last to be hired? Does time matter at all? What is work worth? How do we judge fairness in relation to work and pay? Do socio-economic arguments carry any weight in this context? Are we ever jealous of generosity? Do we make the mistake of misjudging our own worth?

In the marketplace of life's opportunities we are all standing idle, or so it seems with hindsight, until we find the work that really matters to us, that makes sense of our understanding of ourselves, and gives a new purpose to our lives. For some this sense of purpose comes early, some discover it later in life, and others only come to realise what their life means and has meant at the very end. The timing is irrelevant, what matters is that it happens at all. The importance of this realisation or revelation is not measured by longevity. Chronology makes no sense because over time our view of ourselves, and our view of what matters most, changes. Each new realisation is a new start. Each new start is a new opportunity, building on what has happened before, but with new possibilities for our growth as people, and the contribution we can make to the growth of others.

The rewards we enjoy are not in any sense a payment. They are not related to time spent, energy expended, life changes made, help given. We are rewarded by discovering our own value as people. If we think that we are valueless we are not worth anything. Our sense of personal worth dictates our ability, in even the smallest way, to make the world a better place. As each one of us is different, our contribution will be different, and comparison is invidious.

The fact that her skills, talents, and personality are different from his, does not make one "better" or "worse" than the other. There is value in each but we may not have the generosity of spirit to see that. It is therefore entirely reasonable to expect every one of us to be treated the same in the eyes of God. How could it be otherwise?

God's generosity goes beyond our imagination, but because it is universal, and infinite, we cannot be jealous of the way some people appear to benefit in ways that we do not. How do we know? We have no scale with which to weigh or measure. We simply know that just as we are jealous of others, they are equally jealous of us, so what is the point of it all? In our hearts we accept what life has to offer, and in doing so we try to understand what the *kingdom of Heaven* might mean. There is no first or last because we are all trying to understand what we are supposed to be.

Fifteenth Sunday after Trinity
Real Authority

Ezekiel 18:1–4, 25–end Philippians 2:1–13

Psalm 25:1–8 Matthew 21:23–32

If then our common life in Christ yields anything to stir the heart, any consolation of love, any participation in the Spirit, any warmth of affection or compassion, fill up my cup of happiness by thinking and feeling alike, with the same love for one another and a common attitude of mind. Leave no room for selfish ambition and vanity, but humbly reckon others better than yourselves. Look to each other's interests and not merely to your own.

PHILIPPIANS 2:1–4

He entered the temple, and as he was teaching, the chief priests and elders of the nation came up to him and asked, 'By what authority are you acting like this? Who gave you this authority?' Jesus replied, 'I also have question for you. If you answer it, I will tell you by what authority I act. The baptism of John was it from God, or from men?

MATTHEW 21:23–25

This set them arguing among themselves. 'If we say, "From God." He will say, "Then why did you not believe him?" But if we say "From men," we are afraid of the people's reaction, for they all take John for a prophet.' So they answered, 'We do not know.' And Jesus said, 'Then I will not tell you either by what authority I act.'

MATTHEW 21:25–27

Jesus did not suffer fools gladly, particularly those whose view of the world was dictated by rules and regulations. It is not surprising that his response to the chief priests was both challenging and petulant. He was frustrated that the authorities did not realise that he knew that they were trying to catch him out with their question. He was even more irritated that keeping to the rules was all that mattered to them. Proper authorisation of any action was more important than the action itself.

It is one of the great ironies of the Christian faith that over time it has become synonymous with rules of behaviour that run entirely contrary to the liberating message that Jesus preached. The archaic emphasis of "Thou shalt not", aided by a church more ready to forbid than to encourage, has given many people the sense that Christianity is a prescriptive and restrictive religion. This makes people squander their potential and their humanity in rigid adherence to misguided rules for life that dilute enjoyment, make smiles tight-lipped and weaken love. Avoidance of the things that make us human is not a rule for any kind of life.

This negative attitude to life is a simplistic solution to the real problem which is human nature. One size does not fit all. Society requires rules but for most people these are soft touch because they do not feel them. It is only when they become oppressive or petty that people start to notice and react to them.

There will always be those who wilfully break society's rules, and there will always be those for whom small-minded adherence to any rule book gives meaning to their lives. Criminals will in the end receive their just deserts. The petty-minded will not last long. The rest of us often lack the courage of our convictions to know how we should lead our lives. In many of us there is a natural desire to be told what to do. This removes personal responsibility, makes thought unnecessary, and bolsters wavering belief. In the long run however such permission is of dubious value. Who do we trust enough to give us the permission that we feel we need?

The church as an institution has long claimed moral authority over the lives of its adherents, frequently betrayed by its own behaviour and interpretation of what is "right." Churches all too often fail to offer the welcome and support that people need who then leave empty-hearted. We grow out of or rebel against the authority of parents and teachers. We grow into a deeper understanding of what gives an organisation authority we respect because it is a fulfilling place to work, or authority we despise because it is not. We learn to recognise the advice that comes from self-interest, and distrust fair weather friends. We slowly develop the ability to foster long-lasting mutual trust and support in others. That comes from inside us, not from anything we are told to do. In the end, and at the beginning, the permission and the authority has to come from within us.

Jesus' authority was both personal and divine. The two were inextricably and inexplicably combined in a way that those who came into contact with him found it difficult to understand.

As a man he clearly commanded respect and devotion. His behaviour exposed the hypocrisies of society, and he flouted rules that he believed were irrelevant or prohibitive to a dull life. He was a powerful preacher. He knew what he was talking about, and he knew how to inspire those he was talking to. His knowledge of human nature, his view of the temporal and the spiritual world, and his profound sense of his own purpose went beyond human understanding.

It is therefore possible to see another meaning in his response to the church leaders in the temple. He was not prepared to answer their question about his authority because he felt the very ambiguity of his answer would be lost on them or simply misunderstood. For them life was clearly defined by the rules they adhered to. Jesus demonstrated in his life the unity of the material and the spiritual, and by his example he was encouraging all his followers, including ourselves, to discover that for ourselves. We need to discover the inner authority to which others can respond, rather than look for external permission for our behaviour.

Paul in his Letter to the Philippians encourages his readers to see life in this way. He does not, on this occasion, tell his readers what they must or must not do. He does not criticise them for their failures. He does not talk about belief in Christ as an intellectual exercise. He talks about a way of life *in Christ*. This is a life with patterns of behaviour based on humility. It is a way of life that builds love, friendship, warmth, and mutual support. We know instinctively that these are all the things that make life worth living. Our understanding of God comes from our understanding of what is best in human life, an understanding that in Paul's words *stirs the heart*. We do not need any other authority to live life to the full.

Sixteenth Sunday after Trinity

Proper Fruit

Isaiah 5:1–7 Philippians 3:4b–14
Psalm 80:9–17 Matthew 21:33–end

'When they saw the son the tenants said to one another, "This is the heir, come on let us kill him and get his inheritance." So they seized him, flung him out of the vineyard, and killed him. When the owner of the vineyard comes, how do you think he will deal with those tenants?' 'He will bring those bad men to a bad end,' they answered, 'and hand the vineyard over to other tenants, who will give him his share of the crop when the season comes.'

MATTHEW 21:38–41

'Jesus said to them, 'Have you never read the scriptures: "The stone which the builders rejected has become the main corner-stone. This is the Lord's doing, and it is wonderful in our eyes." Therefore I tell you, the kingdom of God will be taken away from you, and given to a nation that yields proper fruit.'

MATTHEW 21:42–43

When the chief priests and Pharisees heard his parables, they saw that he was referring to them. They wanted to arrest him, but were afraid of the crowds, who looked on Jesus as a prophet.

MATTHEW 21:45–46

THE PARABLE OF THE vineyard was the follow-up to Jesus' exchange of with the chief priests and the Pharisees on the question of his authority to preach and teach in the temple. Jesus wanted to drive home their failure to understand who he was and show that he knew what was going to happen to him. They had no difficulty, we are told, in recognising themselves as the bad tenants (though this may be wishful thinking on the part of those who relayed the story.) This realisation however did not dissuade them from their determination to arrest Jesus, the central point of the story, but they were reluctant to do so for fear of a public uprising.

Subsequent events made the meaning of the parable clear, exposing the part that the chief priests and the Pharisees played in Jesus' arrest and execution, and suggesting that they would soon lose all their own authority as religious leaders. God will hand over the world he has created to other spiritual leaders who will have more success in helping people to understand the meaning of their faith and the purpose of their lives.

The parable is easy to understand. It is clear who each of the protagonists is meant to be and what Jesus is trying to tell those who were challenging him. It has a narrative power because we know all too well what was going to happen. Beyond that, does it have any relevance today? I think it does but we need to deconstruct it to reach the inner meaning.

Our life is a very short tenancy in a world that we did not create. We did not have any say in our own creation. Our life is therefore a gift, as is the world in which we live. We even talk about our natural abilities or talents as "gifts." We believe that there is a purpose in all this, though we may have difficulty in understanding what that purpose is. We frequently fail to put our gifts to good use, and we betray our trust as tenants by squandering the earth's resources and destroying the environment. We do this to such an extent that life as we know it may not be sustainable. The future in many parts of the world looks bleak.

Abusing the gifts we have been given is a crime, an affront to the giver. In the privacy of our hearts and minds we are, in some mysterious way, called to account for the way we have lived our lives. We are asked to show a return on the investment we have received. Our own assessment of that return may be grossly inaccurate and inappropriate, but to make sense of our lives we need to think about it.

We can, if we want, put all this to the back of our mind. We can reject all this kind of spiritual analysis as completely irrelevant to the difficult business of making a living. We can turn a deaf ear to the insistent mental knocking of ideas that suggest that there may be more to life than we realise. We can demand more for ourselves because why would anyone want less? We are reluctant to account for anything in our lives for fear that we might be found wanting. If we do all this, we will soon find that the life we want to enjoy shrinks, and we are the poorer.

I also believe we have something to learn from the process Jesus uses to make his point. When challenged with a question about his authority he replied with another question that put the religious leaders in such a quandary that they could not reply. He then refused to respond to their question, and then told a story to expose the current and future meaning of their behaviour.

We are challenged with unsettling questions about our purpose in life, our contribution to society, and whether we are, in the smallest way, making the world we live in a better place. There is never an easy answer. We equivocate, we justify our behaviour on spurious grounds, we excuse our lapses, and we avoid any admission of absolute failure because that would diminish us. In the end we have no real answer to give. As a result of this it is no surprise that when we starting asking profound questions about our life we cannot find any answers either.

To find the answers we need about life we have to be prepared to face difficult questions about the way we live. This will almost always make us depressed and frustrated, because things rarely turn out as well as we would like them to, and we often fail no matter how hard we try. Isaiah felt this keenly:

> *Judge between me and my vineyard. What more could have been done for my vineyard than I did for it? Why, when I expected it to yield choice grapes, did it yield wild grapes?* —Isaiah 5:4

Life is difficult and frustrating. There are no easy answers. It is laborious and challenging work. We will find we have grown many *wild grapes*. Despite that, we all can and will grow *proper fruit* because that is what we are here for.

Seventeenth Sunday after Trinity
Reluctant Guests

Isaiah 25:1–9   Philippians: 4:1–9

Psalm 23   Matthew 22:1–14

The Lord is my shepherd; I lack for nothing. He makes me lie down in green pastures, he leads me to water where I may rest; he revives my spirit; for his name's sake he guides me in the right paths. Even when I walk through a valley of deepest darkness I should fear no harm, for you are with me; your shepherd's staff and crook afford me comfort.

Psalm 23:1–4

The Lord is near; do not be anxious, but in everything make your requests known to God in prayer and petition with thanksgiving. Then the peace of God, which is beyond all understanding, will guard your hearts and your thoughts in Christ Jesus. And now, my friends, all that is true, all that is noble, all that is just and pure, all that is lovable and attractive, whatever is excellent and admirable—fill your thoughts with these things.

Philippians 4:6–8

"The wedding banquet is ready; but the guests I invited did not deserve the honour. Go out, therefore to the main thoroughfares, and invite everyone you can find to the wedding." The servants went out into the streets and collected everyone they could find, good and bad alike. So the hall was packed with guests.

Matthew 22:8–10

THE KINGDOM OF HEAVEN that Jesus describes in the parable of the wedding feast is an uncompromising and brutal place.

The first guests to be invited to the wedding banquet *did not deserve the honour* because they had better things to do. O*ne went off to his farm, another to his business*, and others seized and killed the servants who brought the invitation. The king was so angry that *he sent troops to put those murderers to death and set their town on fire*. Good things follow. Anyone and everyone is invited to the wedding *good and bad alike*, but not everyone has a good time. One guest is not wearing the wedding clothes that we must assume were provided by the host, who is so furious that he *flung him out into the dark, the place of wailing and grinding of teeth*. The moral of the story being that *many are invited, but few are chosen*. What are we to make of all this?

As with the parable of the vineyard, the historical allusions and the echoes of the vengeful God of the Old Testament are easy to recognise. Does it contain any allusions that we can use in our own lives? Our world view is certainly different, as are our expectations of wedding hospitality. The harsher aspects of the story contained echoes that would be more familiar and acceptable to Jesus' audience than they are to us, but we can identify with the anger and frustration of the host whose chosen guests have better things to do with their time than attend his wedding feast.

Jesus' life and teaching offer us a feast of new opportunities to enjoy an entirely different life. This is a life relying on the grace of God that the Psalmist so eloquently describes. He believed, as we are encouraged to believe, that faith in God will give us the support that we need in even the darkest and most difficult times. Paul in his letter to the Philippians voices the same belief. By focusing on what is best in life we will discover the best. This is not as easy as it sounds. It requires commitment from us. In the imagery of the parable, this is wholehearted acceptance of the invitation, not to a short-lived feast but to a different way of life.

Unfortunately, we always have something better to do. There are more real and pressing matters to attend to. Intangible spiritual matters and encouragement to lead a more virtuous life are out of sight and out of mind as we get the children ready for school, shop in Tesco, get the car serviced, attend a Monday morning staff meeting, prepare budgets, pore over a cash flow, or do any of the other important but mundane things that fill our daily life. Our rejection of new ideas may at times be brutal from conscious rejection or mere indifference. Our assumption that the priorities we set in our lives are the right ones may be woefully naïve or short-sighted. We need a very powerful offer to change our view of what really matters in life. Such offers are rare. Things can change in more subtle ways.

There will be times when, unexpectedly or against our better judgement, we find that we are closer to an understanding of what all this means than we think. Something gets under our skin to irritate us. We feel the beginnings of a grudging acceptance that there might be more in all this than meets the eye. This is not a change of heart, but an opening of the mind. We are almost prepared to accept the invitation, but then we discover that we are not ready. We are not mentally prepared. In the words of the parable we are not wearing the right clothes. We are still stuck in the problems of the day to day. We have not found a way to marry the mundane with the spiritual. So near, yet so far. No wonder we feel pain and sorrow.

In our lives there will certainly be moments when we have better things to do than think about how we live and what we believe. We may feel frustrated, troubled, unhappy, and literally aimless as a result. We should not beat ourselves up too much about this. Paul reminds us that we will find peace of mind by making these concerns *known to God in prayer and petition with thanksgiving.*

We need to ask for help in a spirit of thankfulness for what we have, not grievance for what we believe we lack. The *peace of God* is *beyond all understanding* because we know that he knows what we need before we ask for it. Our own understanding will come in the asking.

Our understanding will also come in the moments when we realise that we are just like everyone else. We all, *good and bad alike*, have an opportunity to recognise and experience the best things in life. We will come closer to an understanding of what is *just, pure, lovable, attractive, excellent* and *admirable* that will *revive our spirits* and give us great *comfort*.

Eighteenth Sunday after Trinity
Paying Our Dues

Isaiah 45:1–7   1 Thessalonians 1:1–10
Psalm 96:1–13   Matthew 22:15–22

I am the Lord, and there is none other; apart from me there is no god. Though you have not known me I shall strengthen you, so that from east to west all may know there is none other besides me: I am the Lord, and there is none other; I make the light, I create the darkness; author alike of wellbeing and woe, I, the Lord, do all these things.

Isaiah 45:5–7

'Teacher,' they said, 'we know that you are a sincere man, you teach in all sincerity the way of life that God requires, courting no man's favour, whoever he may be. Give us your ruling on this: are we or are we not permitted to pay taxes to the Roman emperor?'

Matthew 22:16–17

'You hypocrites! Why are you trying to catch me out? Show me a coin used for the tax.' They handed him a silver piece. Jesus asked, 'Whose head is this, and whose inscription?' 'Caesar's,' they replied. He said to them, 'Then pay to Caesar what belongs to Caesar, and to God what belongs to God.' Taken aback by this reply, they went away and left him alone.

Matthew 22:18–22

IN THE TWENTY-FIRST CENTURY, does Jesus' answer to the loaded question about paying taxes have any relevance? I can understand the historical context and appreciate the importance of the question in a country seething with resentment against the Roman occupation. I can see that this is an important moment in the growing antagonism from the religious and secular authorities to Jesus and his teaching. I can enjoy the satisfying neatness of Jesus' answer. I can understand that this goes to the heart of the polarity between the hope that Jesus would lead a physical uprising and his own very different purpose. I can enjoy the fact that he beat his questioners at their own game, and revel in their discomfort. So is this anything more than a good story?

My belief in God and my relationship with him is still for me "work in progress." There are times when I am filled with a surprising certainty. There are many more occasions when I suffer from an indigestion of doubt, perplexity, frustration, and anger that what I feel at some level I would like to believe, at another level seems utterly unbelievable. In those moments Jesus' instruction to *pay to Caesar what belongs to Caesar, and to God what belongs to God*, seems to be confusing, if not meaningless.

I can understand that Jesus is making a distinction between the secular and the spiritual, but the two are inextricably intertwined, so is this separation helpful? Isaiah gives us a powerful reminder that God is everywhere and everything, author of all things, and supporter of all things. In that sense, we belong to him. If that is the case, we *pay to God what belongs to God* by living our lives in a way that is supportive to others, productive to society, personally fulfilling, and spiritually alive. Our payment to God lies in our sensitivity to things that lie beyond our understanding but that we feel have deep importance to why and how we live. All this means that the relevance of Jesus' response lies in the uncertainty that it sets up in my mind. What am I paying, to whom and why?

In the twenty-first century the distinction between the secular (*Caesar*) and the religious *(God)* has become increasingly blurred. It is no longer the case that God is something that some people "do" on Sundays, and then get on with their "normal" life for the rest of the week. Fewer and fewer people, who would if pushed claim to be Christians, "do" God at all. In April 2014 two events brought this into sharp focus.

David Cameron was criticized for referring to the United Kingdom as a "Christian country." The argument was that this ignored both the multifaith nature of our society, and the fact that there were many - humanists, atheists, agnostics, not-interesteds—who took exception to be categorised in this way. No doubt Cameron was expressing both his personal faith and his sense of our national history, but many took exception. A C Grayling, one of the signatories to the original letter of objection, pointed out that Christianity does not have a monopoly on the "kindly attitudes" of tolerance, kindness, and generosity, "characteristics that people of any religion or none can and should have." He went on to say: "It is important in a pluralistic society such as ours that we should not think that uses of 'Christian' to suggest kindly attitudes entail that we are a nation of believers in the dogmas and legends of the religion." (The Times, 26 April 2014)

The second event was that for the first time ever in the UK there were horse race meetings on Good Friday. The horse racing community was delighted. The meetings were well attended. Those who wished to observe Good Friday in some other way were clearly free to do so. I feel sure that there was as much "tolerance, kindness, and generosity" demonstrated at Lingfield Park as there was in any church.

What we owe to God does not lie in Sunday observance or liturgical practice. It is not expressed in a simulated mourning for a barbaric and unjustified execution of an innocent man 2000 years ago, an embarrassed enthusiasm for a resurrection we really do not understand, or even earlier in the year carols for a birth whose grim reality has been coated with the saccharine of sentiment.

What we owe to God lies in acknowledging, sometimes reluctantly, sometimes unexpectedly, that in our day to day life there are brief moments when we see and feel beyond our current experience to something else. What that is remains a mystery and is a paradox. It can give us a profound sense of our own purpose. It can accentuate alienation and a sense of helplessness if we are looking for meaning and we find none.

Fulfilling our daily obligations, like paying taxes to Caesar, is easy. We may feel resentment, suffer some hardship, need to struggle through problems, but at all times we know where and who we are. It is a great deal more difficult to come to terms with what we owe to God. No wonder Isaiah called him *the author of wellbeing and woe*. That's what our life is all about. We owe him both.

Last Sunday after Trinity

Sales Talk

Leviticus 19:1–2, 15–18   1 Thessalonians 2:1–8
Psalm 1   Matthew 22:34–end

Happy is the one who does not take the counsel of the wicked for a guide, or follow the path that sinners tread, or take his seat in the company of scoffers. His delight is in the law of the Lord; it is his meditation day and night. He is like a tree planted beside water channels; it yields its fruit in season and its foliage never fades. So he too prospers in all he does.

Psalm 1:1–3

When we preach, we do not curry favour with men; we seek only the favour of God, who is continually testing our hearts. We have never resorted to flattery, as you have cause to know; nor, as God is our witness, have our words ever been a cloak for greed. We have never sought honour from men, not from you or from anyone else, although as Christ's own envoys we might have made our weight felt; but we were as gentle with you as a nurse caring for her children.

1 Thessalonians 2:4–7

'Teacher, which is the greatest commandment in the law?' He answered, '"Love the Lord your God with all your heart, with all your soul, and with all your mind." That is the greatest, the first commandment. The second is like it, "Love your neighbor as yourself." Everything in the law and the prophets hangs on these two commandments.'

Matthew 22:36–40

Selling does not get a good press. No matter how excellent their product or service, or how well meaning they are personally, sales people are all too often regarded as foot-in-the-door charlatans who use deceptive and flattering sales talk to persuade us to buy things we don't want and certainly don't need.

Sales people took some time to address this prejudice. Many years ago, the training courses I attended were focused on "closing the deal", with templates for sales talk that would trap the unwary into commitments to buy before they had comes to terms with what was on sale. This merely enhanced the pariah status of the selling profession. Three things changed this: understanding the buyer, redefining the product, and providing a new kind of service.

There was a growing recognition that buyers were not stupid, they knew what they wanted and could make rational decisions which made any sales trickery counterproductive. Blinding them with an endless recitation of product features would get nowhere. They needed to understand how the product would help them do what they had to do. Nothing else mattered. This transformed the salesman or the saleswoman from an unwelcome irritant into someone who could genuinely help because they understood the buyer and could provide solutions to his or her problems and needs.

Preaching is selling, but is it merely a repetition of product features or a presentation of benefits that is really focused on the buyers' needs?

Paul in his Letter to the Thessalonians is at pains to set out his own and his readers' credentials as preachers. They are behaving in the right way in God's eyes, and though they have divine authority to be heavy handed with their message, they have nurtured and cared for their audience to ensure full understanding and acceptance. Does this reflect the nature of preaching today?

The problem with "selling" Christianity is that the Bible is such an unhelpful product manual. Over long, contradictory, confusing, with conflicting messages about the nature of God, and dubious and unsubstantiated claims about the benefits that will accrue to us when we have stopped living. Not a good offer.

I am told that good behaviour is its own reward, because life will be better, but that the true reward will come later, in heaven. This is a concept that quickly defies belief as it requires an understanding of the nature of God who is unknowable. Why would I buy into this fantasy? I am told that such doubts are quite natural, but what I need is faith. I am asked to recognise the product benefits without really understanding what the product is, how it works, and why it is important for me.

This is difficult stuff to sell, and my frustration is that much talk from the pulpit is an unsatisfactory repetition of details from the product manual, with generalised explanations that fail to get under the surface of the story or under the skin of the listeners. A continuous series of stories that encourage moral rectitude and a catalogue of good behaviour is boring. It is little more than a painting-by-numbers set. Put the right colours in the right places it will all make sense, but what happens if I do not like the picture?

The Psalmist recommends a pattern of good behaviour and paints his own picture of the well-watered tree to make the point that this is the way to live a fulfilling life. The sanctity of the Old Testament does not give this any particular authority, but it does prompt us to wonder, if we are so inclined, whether that might be true. The artist paints a complex picture whose meaning will be found only in our willingness to look and react to it.

Jesus, I believe, recognised that his preaching was going to last, and the longer it lasted, the more profound its effect would be. He knew that this would only be achieved if the truth that he preached required and demanded further thought. Its simplicity was deceptive. The words of his two great commandments are easy to understand, but their true meaning is unique to each individual.

So what do I want? I want a preacher who recognises the uniqueness of my response (and of everyone else) to what I am hearing. A preacher who seeks to aid difficulties of understanding without resorting to academic explanations. A preacher who focuses on the personal. A preacher who offers guidance on how I might think about life, without prescribing how I should live. I want to be sold ideas that I can believe in because they stimulate my appetite for something more profound that I might really want to buy.

All Saints Day
Personal Failures

Revelation 7:9–end   1 John 3:1–3

Psalm 34:1–10   Matthew 5:1–12

Dear friends, we are now God's children; what we shall be has not yet been disclosed, but we know that when Christ appears we shall be like him, because we shall see him as he is. As he is pure, everyone who has grasped this hope makes himself pure.

1 JOHN 3:2–3

'Blessed are the poor in spirit; the kingdom of Heaven is theirs. Blessed are the sorrowful; they shall find consolation. Blessed are the gentle; they shall have the earth for their possession. Blessed are those who hunger and thirst to see right prevail; they shall be satisfied.'

MATTHEW 5:3–6

'Blessed are those who show mercy; mercy shall be shown to them. Blessed are those whose hearts are pure; they shall see God. Blessed are the peacemakers; they shall be called God's children. Blessed are those who are persecuted in the cause of right; the Kingdom of Heaven is theirs.

MATTHEW 5:7–10

PERSONAL FAILURES

For most of my life I read and heard the well-known words of the Sermon on the Mount in a haze of good feelings. Jesus is talking about an ideal world where good things happen and where good people thrive. This was something I could recognise and in a Sunday mood of acquiescence accept as a template for living. Life however is tougher than that because human nature goes in the opposite direction. Far from being a soft-focus catalogue of good behaviour, Jesus' words are an indictment of my failings as a person. Jesus exposes how far we all fall short of any ideal, and how the world we create as a result is anything but *blessed*.

I wrestle with the question, do we think of ourselves as inherently good, or inherently bad? I must immediately admit that I have no belief in original sin. I do not believe that all humans have some germ of badness implanted in their character, and that they are in any sense fundamentally evil. That would make nonsense of any concept of free will. It would also compel us to pursue ridiculous arguments about how we might kill or remove this germ, and inoculate—perhaps we should say indoctrinate—ourselves to prevent its return.

I do believe however that living a *pure* life is very difficult, and in the long run not much fun. There are times, rare for some, frequent for others, when we choose the dark rather than the light. Those are the times when we revel in the illicit, are attracted by excess and repelled by abstinence. Jesus knew that this was one of the grim facts of human nature. Outspoken condemnation would do little to change something that was so deeply ingrained in all of us. He recognised that we need to brought face to face with reality of our frequent failures, and he did so by pointing to their opposite.

The Sermon on the Mount asks whether we are *poor in spirit, sorrowful, gentle,* eager to pursue what is *right,* capable of showing *mercy, pure in heart, peacemakers,* willing to suffer for the things we believe in. This list challenges us all to ask, "Is this me?" and to be embarrassed by the answers that we give.

It is interesting that *poor in spirit* is first on the list. I have heard this interpreted as meaning humble, not full of self or selfish interests, not interested in worldly matters and therefore open to what God is offering us. I have also heard more extreme interpretations that suggest the phrase emphasises are spiritual worthlessness, and therefore our need for God. All this for me is far too negative, and seems to be at odds with what follows.

Jesus recognised, and was frequently exasperated by his disciples' inability to grasp his spiritual message. They could not see beyond the day to day and their material expectations of Jesus' life. They failed to appreciate the new way of thinking and the new way of living that he was offering. We have the same problem. I believe that we are all *poor in spirit* because by our very nature our understanding of spiritual matters is limited and inadequate. Right at the start of his sermon Jesus is saying that is not in itself a barrier to a growing understanding of our purpose in God's world.

It is very easy to beat ourselves up about our failures, to bemoan the poverty of our spiritual lives, to mourn the fact that open-hearted belief has been destroyed by other interests. The church's emphasis on the negatives of our personal failings simply makes matters worse. We are therefore sorrowing people, who need the consolation of knowing that we are not all bad.

We live in a very aggressive and acquisitive society. Gentle is not an adjective we use very often about ourselves or our family, friends and colleagues. We know what gentleness is, and we yearn for it, but we fear that it is not a passport to the success that we want. That is not to say that our behaviour is harsh, belligerent, unfeeling, cruel, and callous. It is just that we are often not as gentle to others as we would like them to be to us. We are not kind because we respond in kind.

Our intentions are good. We believe in what is right, and we would like goodness, and justice, and fairness, and honesty to prevail always and everywhere. We cannot personally change the world, but we need to ask whether, in our own small way, we do enough to make the change that we want to see happen. Are we hungry enough to make good things happen?

We will help to change the world if we show compassion and forgiveness to everyone. Mercy as a word has fallen out of fashion, but compassion has taken its place. We need to explore our ability to understand other people, whoever and wherever they are, and ensure that we treat them as we would like them to treat us. This will help us develop a new purity of heart because we are focused on the ultimate good for the world. This the First Letter of John sees as a reflection of Jesus. This will bring peace. This is the modern *cause of right,*

If we use the Sermon on the Mount as a personal questionnaire, to call ourselves to account, we will have the acute sense that much as we would like to be blessed or happy, we still have some way to go before that happens.

Fourth Sunday before Advent
Ends and Beginnings

Micah 3:5–end   1 Thessalonians 2:9–13
Psalm 43   Matthew 24:1–14

'Take care that no one misleads you. For many will come claiming my name and saying, "I am the Messiah," and many will be misled by them. The time is coming when you will hear of wars and rumours of wars. See that you are not alarmed. Such things are bound to happen; but the end is still to come.'

Matthew 24:4–6

'Nation will go to war against nation, kingdom against kingdom; there will be famines and earthquakes in many places. All these things are the first birth-pangs of the new age. You will then be handed over for punishment and execution; all nations will hate you for your allegiance to me. At that time many will fall from their faith; they will betray one another and hate one another.'

Matthew 24:7–10

'Many false prophets will arise, and will mislead many; and as lawlessness spreads, the love of many will grow cold. But whoever endures to the end will be saved. And this gospel of the kingdom will be proclaimed throughout the earth as testimony to all nations; and then the end will come.'

Matthew 24:11–14

Jesus was talking to the disciples about the destruction of the temple in Jerusalem. They, literal-minded as always, had asked him exactly when this would take place as they linked it with Jesus' Second Coming and *the end of the age.* They must have had mixed feelings about this. No wonder they were anxious.

The Second Coming was clearly something to look forward to, but it required Jesus to end his life on earth first which they did not want to think about. The *end of the age* was a horrifying prospect, particularly if it included the divine destruction of huge buildings, but Jesus had given them hope that at this moment they would enter a new relationship with God, the ultimate fulfilment of their lives.

Jesus did little to soothe or unravel their confused feelings. He painted a bleak picture of the future which gave the disciples very little to look forward to, leaving the real nature of *the end* tantalising and ambiguous. It is easy to identify with the disciples who heard apocalyptic stories about the end of the world as they knew it and wanted to know when it was all going to happen. Jesus was at pains to curb their impatience by emphasising that many difficult and painful things were going to happen in the world and to them first. That was where their attention should be focused. The immediate future was more important than an end that was beyond their, and our, understanding of human life and time. I believe that we need the same reality check to avoid trying to interpret life from the perspective of what we believe may happen at its end. Our fanciful notions of 'heavenly rewards' will not help us to sort out the problems of the here and now. A different perspective will.

Looking forward we hope for good things in a world we cannot imagine. Looking back with the illusory benefit of hindsight we see immaturity, youthful ignorance, and missed opportunities. We reinterpret our personal history to give the events in our lives a pattern and cohesion that makes sense of our lives now. We want it all to make sense, but the bitter truth is that we can only hope that it will, rather than believe that it does.

Life is a succession of endings. We give names to the stages in our lives, childhood, adolescence, middle age, but we are never quite sure where one stopped and the other began. The older we get the more we talk about feeling younger in our hearts than our calendar years. We feel as if we are making steady progress in getting older from one calendar year to the next. The older we get the wiser we hope we are, but looking back the more ignorant we feel we were. In retrospect our steady progress across the years merges into stages in our life, periods when we were this, and periods when we were that. We can recall personal rites of passage that mark a succession of endings, and a succession of new beginnings.

Jesus' words to his disciples have a relevance for us in the way we think about the stages in our life and about our life as whole. There will always be hints of disaster from any number of sources. Life never goes smoothly. We must be prepared for that. We must take the long view and believe that in our own lives while things may not often be as good as we hoped, they will rarely be as bad as we feared.

On the other hand Jesus' summary of what the disciples can expect in the wider world is the stuff of our modern news bulletins. Wars, famines, earthquakes, persecution, death, betrayals, and religious hatred are just a small part of the catalogue of daily horrors. It is difficult for us to see these as *the first birth-pangs of a new age*, or to take any comfort from the fact that they might be. It seems ridiculously complacent to suggest that no matter how horrific are world events, it will all come right in the end. We cannot imagine what "come right" would mean. We cannot imagine what that "end" might be.

The only way that we can cope is to focus on the purpose of our own lives. This is not a selfish or self-centred strategy. It grows out of a belief we cannot change the whole world. We cannot bring peace to the Middle East, feed the hungry, prevent global warming, stop child abuse, and house the homeless. What we can do is any number of small things that will contribute to all of that, and to the happiness of all those around us.

It is the small personal crusades that are difficult to sustain. It is easy to be persuaded by the *false prophets* that the little things that we do are just too small to matter. As life becomes more difficult, and new problems arise we will certainly lose heart. Little by little we learn that if we pursue difficult challenges to the end, rewards will come. Those rewards are a new start. In T.S.Eliot's words from *East Coker* "In my end is my beginning."

Third Sunday before Advent
Be Prepared

Amos 5:18–24 1 Thessalonians 4:13–end
Psalm 70 Matthew 25:1–13

'When the day comes, the kingdom of Heaven will be like this. There were ten girls, who took their lamps and went out to meet the bridegroom. Five of them were foolish, and five prudent; when the foolish ones took their lamps they took no oil with them, but the others took flasks of oil with their lamps.'

MATTHEW 25:1–4

'The foolish said to the prudent, "Our lamps are going out; give us some of your oil." "No," they answered, "there will never be enough for all of us. You had better go to the dealers and buy some for yourselves."'

MATTHEW 25:8–9

'While they were away the bridegroom arrived; those who were ready went in with him to the wedding banquet; and the door was shut. Later the others came back. "Sir, sir, open the door for us," they cried. But he answered, "Truly I tell you: I do not know you." Keep awake then, for you know neither the day nor the hour.'

MATTHEW 25:10–13

BE PREPARED

IT IS POSSIBLE TO argue that in what is normally called the Parable of the Ten Virgins Jesus is talking about his Second Coming, and that he is the bridegroom, who will judge our behaviour at that time with dire consequences if we are found wanting in any way. I personally do not find this in any way helpful.

I have difficulty with the whole idea of the Second Coming. Is this the moment when somehow, somewhere way Jesus will reappear to carry on the work he began two thousand years ago? There is no question that the world has more need of him now than it did then. It is equally without question that even with a global reach via modern technology his task would be infinitely harder. Skepticism would quickly lead to rejection. He would come to an ignominious end or die at the hands of a fanatic, in both cases a mere footnote to yesterday's news. Why come at all?

It is no easier to believe that the Second Coming is another way of describing the Day of Judgement when the good and the bad will be chosen and separated? I have always believed that "judgement" is happening now. It makes no sense to me to imagine some kind of heavenly law court, where we are called to account for our sins and are then summarily "sent down" or released. Our creation and our relationship with a loving God demands something entirely different.

The whole tenor of our lives is a continuous up and down process of learning and understanding, failure and success, progress and frustration. Our ability to cope with this mixture of conviction and uncertainty is the way we are challenged to make the most of our lives. This is not in response to any divine instruction, though some may find it helpful to think like that. It is not so that at the end of our lives we receive "good results" in the final examination of our life. It is a self-evident truth that we should make the best use of the life we have been given. If we do not, we have only ourselves to blame, so the "judgement" is in our hands. In my mind therefore, judgement and selection are not about our ultimate fate, and being called to account. It is far more personal and immediate.

The lamp without oil is a useful image. Setting out the girls were in high spirits, as we so often are. They knew where they were going and this was exciting. They could see their way, until the oil ran out. They looked for help from their friends who were far too busy with their own affairs. They had to look elsewhere for the oil they needed and as a result they arrived late and were harshly rejected because they had failed to live up to expectations.

This is a hard lesson to learn. Do we see enough, do we know enough, do we understand ourselves enough to be ready for what life has to offer?

The key sentence in the parable is the last: *Keep awake then, for you know neither the day nor the hour.* In our own lives we do not know how or when we will be faced with unique opportunities to look at the world in a new way. This can change everything in our lives. We need to be alert to these new possibilities. We may not even recognise them as opportunities because we are so wrapped up in our current way of life and our short term ambitions. We may simply ignore them because they require great effort or take us down an unexpected path. We can easily reject them because we are just not ready. We therefore miss a chance to realise our potential. We are not the people we could be. That is why the bridegroom says, *"Truly I tell you; I do not know you."*

This is a continuous process, not a single event. We owe it to ourselves to think about the consequences of any action or any inaction. We also owe it to ourselves to follow what we think might be the right course, even if we are not sure why. There are risks involved, but life is full of them. We limit who we are by avoiding the risks that could define what we can be.

The judgement in and on our lives is the regret that we feel at an opportunity missed, a path not taken, advice ignored, encouragement dismissed, praise rejected, or love squandered. We bemoan something lost for ever that could have made an infinite difference to who we are and what we do. We cannot afford to allow that to happen.

We need to be awake to the inner voice that tells us that the course of action we like least is the right one to take. We need to be awake to the voices of others who see in us something we do not recognise ourselves. We need to be awake to the things that give us the greatest pleasure and satisfaction. We need to be awake to the lessons of dissatisfaction to learn what need in us is not being met. We need to be awake to what really matters in our lives. We need to be awake to what we believe. We need to be awake to the fact that the day and the hour could be now.

Second Sunday before Advent
Hidden Talents

Zephaniah 1:7, 12–end   I Thessalonians 5:1–11
Psalm 90:1–8   Matthew 25:14–30

'Then the man who had been given one bag came and said. "Master, I knew you to be a hard man; you reap where you have not sown, you gather where you have not scattered; so I was afraid, and I went and hid your gold in the ground. Here it is—you have what belongs to you."

MATTHEW 25:24–25

"You worthless, lazy servant," said the master. "You knew, did you, that I reap where I have not sown, and gather where I have not scattered? Then you ought to have put my money on deposit, and on my return I should have got it back with interest. Take the bag of gold from him, and give it to the one with ten bags."

MATTHEW 25:26–28

"For everyone who has will be given more, till he has enough and to spare; and everyone who has nothing will forfeit even what he has. As for the useless servant, throw him into the dark, where there will be wailing and grinding of teeth!"

MATTHEW 25:29–30

THE FAMILIARITY OF THE parables Jesus told breeds a nodding acceptance of their truth without much conviction that their various meanings have any immediate relevance. They become pleasing moral fables, with the odours of sanctity and childhood, out of touch with what is really going on in our lives. Some however have a harshness and bitterness that strike a different note and command attention. The Parable of the Talents, as it is usually called, is one of those.

This Parable comes immediately after the Parable of the Ten Virgins (see Third Sunday before Advent). Both are challenging descriptions of the nature of the "kingdom of heaven." Jesus is offering encouragement, hope and a dire warning. He wants to gives his disciples tools to spread his message. He wants to give them, and their followers, new ways to think about "the kingdom of heaven", the new world order that they will discover through belief in him. He wants to drive the message home by looking forward to a day of judgement when we will be called to account for our lives and the use of the talents, our "natural aptitudes and skills" (OED) that we have been given. This gives the story its immediacy today.

On the surface this could be a parable for our times in other ways. It is a story of skilful investment, money making money, to please an investor whose sole purpose was maximising his return. Those who did well, are recognised, and rewarded with an additional bonus; the one who did not, is criticised, abused, and dismissed, to find himself among the have-nots of society. This is not however a simple and prophetic tale of Wall Street and the City of London.

Each servant is given money based on his abilities. This is not a random share out, but a carefully considered matching process. The amount of money given to each is enormous. Scholars suggest that a talent was the equivalent of twenty years work by an ordinary person. This is no idle investment. The owner goes away for a long period, more than enough time for the servants to make the best possible use of the money they have been given.

The servant who did nothing at all with the money he was given misunderstands his master's purpose and claims that he did what he did out of fear. This is the vengeful and angry God of the Old Testament overriding the message that Jesus was at pains to make clear. The servant had been indoctrinated with an idea of God that was entirely inappropriate. This had narrowed his view of life to one of unimaginative obedience. He was afraid what might happen to him, and to avoid punishment did nothing. At face value this appears to be a feeble and counter-intuitive excuse. As the master says, the sensible thing would have been simply to put the money in the bank, and let it earn interest there. The human condition is not always so rational.

Fear is exactly the reason why we do not use our talents to the full. We lack confidence, we wilt under peer pressure, we are nervous at putting our ideas forward, and we are worried about the opinion of those in authority over us. We do the basics of what has to be done because we think that is the safest path. It is a poor strategy to choose. Under-achievement breeds more of the same. We lose our way, and very probably our job.

As the Parable of the Ten Virgins shows, the greater loss is the failure to use the opportunities we are unexpectedly given. We will experience life-changing consequences if we fail to create significantly more with the gifts or talents that we have been given. Life is short. If we do not use our talents to the full, time will run out on us. We will lose the talents and therefore the opportunities that we have, leaving us nothing but regrets, which are no more than an investment in negativity. We will feel even more pain when we see others investing their talents thoughtfully, doing more with their lives in ways that they never imagined, and seizing opportunities that could have been ours.

We need the courage of our convictions and our belief in ourselves to make the most of what we have and who we are. Our talents are unique to us, they are part of the mix that makes us what we are. We can invest our talents in a way that fills the whole of our life and makes sense of it, or we can squander them in a way that makes less of them and of us. It is our job in life to make the best use of them. If we use our talents to the full we will be recognised and rewarded (materially, intellectually and emotionally), and we will learn what our unique purpose in life really is.

We all need to ask ourselves ten questions. These are so important that we need to spend time thinking about the answers. We cannot afford to do less. What do I enjoy doing most and why? What talents have I been given? What talents do I have that others recognise more than I do? Which of these talents am I investing in things that matter? Which talents am I squandering in things that don't? Am I using my talents to the full in the work that I am doing or the life that I am leading? How could I use my talents better? What would happen if I did? What is stopping me? What am I afraid of?

Sunday next before Advent

Touching God

Ezekiel 34:11–16, 20–24 Ephesians 1:15–end
Psalm 144:1–7 Matthew 25:31– end

Lord, what are human beings that you should care for them? What are frail mortals that you should take thought for them? They are no more than a puff of wind, their days like a fleeting shadow.

Psalm 144:3–4

'Then the righteous will reply, "Lord, when was it that we saw you hungry and fed you, or thirsty and gave you drink, a stranger and took you home, or naked and clothed you? When did we see you ill or in prison, and come to visit you?"

Matthew 25:37–39

"Truly I tell you: anything you did for one of my brothers here, however insignificant, you did for me."

Matthew 25:40

This is the last Sunday of the Christian year. The passages for the three previous Sundays have demanded a close and uncomfortable look at what the future might hold and what the "kingdom of heaven" might mean for the disciples and each one of us. We now have a more intimate reality check. Our insignificance in relation to what we think about God is contrasted with the very personal way in which we might have a relationship with him now. Not through struggles to find the right words to talk about the indescribable. Not through any extremes of liturgical practice. Not through adherence to any ultra-strict codes of behaviour. Not through conscientious avoidance of anything that is morally dubious. Not through excessive confession of minor and irrelevant lapses that hardly deserve the name "sin." We discover him by helping others.

The things that make us fully human, the things that make everyone's life better, the things that improve society, the things that make life here and now worth living, are the very things that give us a glimpse, a sensation, an inkling of what God might be. This for me is the ultimate paradox. It cuts through all other arguments. It throws us back on ourselves, to ask in our own way *"When was it that we saw you hungry and fed you?"*

The danger for me in all this is that we take Jesus' words too literally and focus on "good deeds" as the way to know God. Even if we half-believe this is true we run the risk of making "charitable work" an end in itself. We do it because we believe it is a good thing to do. Because it is a good thing to do it will make us good. Because we are good we are among "the sheep." Because we are among "the sheep" God will smile on us. This is a spurious and romantic argument that makes little sense.

I am left with the question that has troubled so many, "How do I find God?" Does the answer lie in others? Through my behaviour towards others? In experiences that lift my heart? With the help of those further along the same path? Through the teaching of Jesus? The questions presuppose that there is an answer. I am no longer sure that there is. More accurately, I am no longer sure that there is an answer that I would recognise as an appropriate response to the question I have asked. If God is beyond question and beyond understanding there can be no answer. Does that leave me helpless or hopeful?

I am hopeful because language and words can only do so much, and that is never enough. Because of this Jesus used stories, parables, images, and personal challenges to persuade his followers to think differently. They struggled. We are still struggling despite the wisdom of many and centuries of experience. I would not be asking the question if others had found the answer. Our words, and those of many before us are helpful, yet inconclusive. They point us in a particular direction but do not take us the whole way.

I have difficulty with time—the eternal nature of God. I have difficulty with space—the ubiquity of God. I have difficulty with the relationship—the love of God. I have difficulty with meaning—the purpose of God. I have difficulty with trust—the unknowable nature of God. I have difficulty with all these because I cannot translate them into my life except as an intricate, intellectual exercise that fulfils no real purpose. For that reason it is helpful to exclude what I cannot understand.

It is also helpful to define the limits of language. "Finding God" is not a question of movement. It is not a question of location. It is not a question that can be answered by any of the prepositions. There is no "to", "by", "with", "from", or "through" in the understanding of God. If he is, he is, and he is all that is.

Paul in his Letter to the Romans, quoting from Old Testament sources puts it better:

> *How deep are the wealth and the wisdom and the knowledge of God! How inscrutable his judgements, how unsearchable his ways! 'Who knows the mind of the Lord? Who has been his counsellor?' 'Who has made a gift to him first and earned a gift in return?' From him and through him and for him all things exist—to him be glory for ever! Amen.* —Romans 11:33–36

It has taken me a long time to come to terms with belief in the importance of life as the essential and fundamental ingredient of belief in God. Faith in an ultimate revelation, a life after death, a second coming, a day of judgement, a final accounting, a new world takes me away from life into "the beyondness of things." There is value in thinking beyond life, but only if it helps us to understand life itself, and why we are here.

This for me is the real meaning of Jesus' emphasis on the importance of *"anything you did for one of my brothers here, however insignificant, you did for me."* Doing anything, now, for others, be it thinking, helping, encouraging, comforting, loving, caring, and receiving the same from them, with thanks, grace and gratitude, these are the things that really matter because they are what God is.

Conclusions

Overview

OVER THE LAST SIX months I have read the 240 passages from the Bible appointed for each Sunday and major Feast Day in 2014. I have selected 500 verses that made an immediate impact on me, and I have written short 'sermons' to myself to explore why those particular verses were for me important. I did this as honestly and objectively as I could, relying entirely on my own knowledge, understanding and interpretation. I wanted to see whether using Bible passages as a starting point would help me to clarify and articulate my own Christian beliefs. I now need to take stock.

There were many surprises in the whole process, not least in the many unexpected connections between the verses I had chosen. I was struck anew, as if for the first time, by the powerful simplicity of the Gospel accounts of Jesus' life and teaching. I needed to find ways to get inside each story to find interpretations that made sense to me. At the same time I was struck by how much I read did not strike any chord at all and was a distraction. Despite this my initial skepticism diminished as conviction grew. This left the conversion of a newly discovered truth into meaningful behaviour as the main problem. I was left with the pleasing uncertainty that I was a little closer to God.

Surprises

I approached the passages I had selected with no preconceptions. I responded to the words and imagery of each passage and to some sense of their meaning. I had no idea in advance of what I was going to say about them. Each chapter was an entirely new and self-contained experience. The surprise was that no matter how bereft of ideas I felt at the start of each piece of writing, ideas always came. Sometimes this happened quickly, sometimes sluggishly, but they always came. More often than not, what I was writing felt all too obvious and mundane, but then blossomed into interpretations that were, for me, unexpected and helpful. It was a cumulative process of discovering and understanding. One thought led to another. I felt that I was moving forward, even though I was not sure where I was heading.

Connections

At the start I had made an entirely arbitrary decision to choose three sets of verses to think about in each chapter. Sometimes these three were spread across the Old Testament, the Gospels, and the Epistles. Sometimes there were just Gospels and Epistles. Towards the end, almost entirely from the Gospels, which in the readings set for 2014 meant Matthew. In passages from the Gospels it was important for me to capture the essence of a situation or a parable, so passages were consecutive. Where the passages came from three different parts of the Bible I was surprised by the connections that I discovered between verses with disparate themes and audiences. These connections were particularly illuminating.

Powerful simplicity

I have found many times when exploring the readings that it was the simplest details that were often the most revealing. The nuance of a reply. A sudden burst of irritation. An emotional response. Tears of sadness or of joy. The realities of day to day life taking precedence over the spiritual. The ambiguity of language giving breadth of meaning to simple words. It did not take me long to recognise that Jesus was the central figure in all these moments. This was something of a shock. I had started out, I realised, with an inner prejudice about Jesus. I wanted to avoid "Jesus talk", and I was confused, as I still am, whether I should refer to him as Jesus, Christ, or Jesus Christ. His person and the personality grew in importance to me. I recognised, from his attitude to his disciples and others, that he understood human nature and human needs better than we do ourselves.

CONCLUSIONS

Storytelling

In the Foreword, I was scathing about the pulpit habit of retelling Bible stories rather than interpreting them. I had to eat my words. I found that there is little need to repeat Bible stories in a modern idiom to bring out their sense as a story. It is however vitally important to get inside the story, to understand emotional drivers, to recognise areas of conflict, to empathise with doubts, as it is through these that real, immediate meaning merges.

Valid interpretation

There were moments when I was concerned at my arrogance and presumption. How could I claim any validity for my interpretations which had no basis in scholarship or the simplest academic study? Would my understanding of a particular passage be completely negated by the discovery that the words to which I was responding meant something different in Hebrew, Greek, or Aramaic? I complained at the start that academic unravelling of that kind was not always helpful. The words, in any translation, have their own power and impact. We would not still be reading them if that was not the case. My response therefore, unfettered by the explanations of others, was valid in its own right. I was one with a silent community of struggling believers who are facing the same problems of finding interpretations that have personal meaning.

Other readings

My selection of verses amounts to less than 20% of all the readings appointed in the Lectionary. This is not surprising when I am selecting by subjective impact. It is worth thinking about where I had problems with the other 80%. I found it very difficult to respond to most of the Old Testament passages. If I had been in the mood I might have found them historically interesting, but this was not my focus of attention. I found it very difficult to relate them to my thinking and understanding today. Explaining their historical context and importance as background to the New Testament does not help. I had expected to respond more positively to the poetry of the Psalms, but I became weary of endless praise and breast-beating self-abasement. With some notable exceptions, the Epistles became equally wearisome. Moral exhortation to endure persecution for infinite and indefinable rewards gave me cause for concern, not hope. I found that the passages that did not strike any chord were a distraction from those that did.

Removing skepticism

I had started writing in the hope that the process of exploration would remove my doubts, and increase my conviction. I hoped for a positive result because I was dissatisfied with the limbo of uncertainty about what I believed. I was predisposed to want to believe but deeply skeptical, after years of religious flirtation, that anything meaningful would emerge. To begin with I was even hedging my bets by telling myself that if a verse or an idea began to make sense to me, that was my upbringing and my education talking, not my adult self. I soon came to the conclusion that this self-doubt was counterproductive. Why not allow conviction to grow on its own terms?

Growing conviction

Conviction did grow. I became more and more certain that this process meant something and that accepting that was more valuable than believing that it meant nothing. I was challenged again and again to ask whether believing the truth of an idea automatically made me a better person or the world a better place. The answer was usually that it did not. The difficulty was and is how to convert that truth into something that makes sense in my life. I do not have the answer to that yet. I do know however that the value of the truth will not go away and that understanding will only come through living. Staying with the truth is what matters.

Concluding uncertainty

Finally, and most potently, I was surprised by the extraordinary uncertainty that surrounds believing the Christian message and understanding the Christian life. Faith is supposed to be the antidote to uncertainty, yet faith is itself uncertain. I found that understanding and meaning were elusive, hovering on the edge of my intellectual vision. I could almost see them. I could almost grasp them. It left me wondering whether the "almost" is where God is.

Index of Bible Extracts

Acts 1:9-11	97	Isaiah 53:7	76
Acts 2:1-4	103	Isaiah 55:10-11	118
Acts 2:40-41	85	Isaiah 58:6-7	37
Acts 10:39-41	79	James 5:7-8	7
Acts 17:26-28	94	Jeremiah 20:9	109
1 Corinthians 1:7-9	28	Jeremiah 28:8-9	112
1 Corinthians 1:17	31	1 John 3:2-3	166
1 Corinthians 2:9-11	37	John 1:1-5	13
1 Corinthians 3:1-3	40	John 1:10-11	19
1 Corinthians 3:5-9	40	John 1:14	19
1 Corinthians 11:23-26	73	John 1:35-37	28
1 Corinthians 12:4-7	103	John 3:7-8	55
1 Corinthians 12:8-10	103	John 3:16-17	55
2 Corinthians 5:21	50	John 4:13-15	58
2 Corinthians 6:6-7	49	John 4:24-26	60
2 Corinthians 6:8-10	51	John 4:32-34	58
Ephesians 1:17-18	97	John 9:24-25	64
Exodus 24:18	46	John 9:30-32	64
Genesis 1:1	43	John 10:7-11	88
Genesis 3:2-5	52	John 11:25-26	67
Genesis 3:6-7	52	John 11:33-35	67
Hebrews 1:3-4	13	John 11:36-37	67
Hebrews: 2:17-18	16	John 13:13-15	73
Isaiah 5:4	156	John 13:34-35	73
Isaiah 9:2	31	John 14:2-4	91
Isaiah 11:2-5	4	John 14:5-7	91
Isaiah 11:6-8	4	John 14:8-10	91
Isaiah 11:9	5	John 14:15-17	94
Isaiah 35:5-7	7	John 14:19-21	94
Isaiah 40:12-15	106	John 17:6-8	100
Isaiah 40:29-31	108	John 18:37-38	76
Isaiah 42:1-4	25	John 20:14-16	79
Isaiah 45: 5-7	160	John 20:17-18	79

INDEX OF BIBLE EXTRACTS

John 20:24-25	82	Matthew 17:5-8	46
John 20:26-29	82	Matthew 18:20	142
1 Kings 3:9-12	124	Matthew 18:21-22	145
1 Kings 19:11-13	130	Matthew 18:32-35	145
Luke 1:30-32	61	Matthew 19:29-30	31
Luke 1:34-35	61	Matthew 20:1-4	148
Luke 1:38	61	Matthew 20:8-10	148
Luke 2:34-35	34	Matthew 20:11-16	148
Luke 18:16	134	Matthew 21:6-8	70
Luke 24:13-16	85	Matthew 21:23-25	151
Luke 24:30-32	85	Matthew 21:25-27	151
Luke 24:50-53	97	Matthew 21:38-41	154
Malachi 3:5	34	Matthew 21:42-43	154
Matthew 1:18-19	10	Matthew 21:45-46	154
Matthew 1:20-21	10	Matthew 22:8-10	157
Matthew 2:1-2	22	Matthew 22:16-17	160
Matthew 2:8	22	Matthew 22:18-22	160
Matthew 2:11-12	22	Matthew 22:36-40	163
Matthew 2:13-15	16	Matthew 24:4-6	169
Matthew 3:13-15	25	Matthew 24:7-10	169
Matthew 3:16-17	25	Matthew 24:11-14	169
Matthew 4:1	52	Matthew 24:42-43	1
Matthew 5:3-6	166	Matthew 24:44	1
Matthew 5:7-10	166	Matthew 25:1-4	172
Matthew 5:13-15	37	Matthew 25:8-9	172
Matthew 5:29-30	40	Matthew 25:10-13	172
Matthew 6:1	49	Matthew 25:24-25	175
Matthew 6:25-27	43	Matthew 25:26-28	175
Matthew 6:33-34	43	Matthew 25:29-30	175
Matthew 7:7	xiii	Matthew 25:37-39	178
Matthew 10:29-30	109	Matthew 25:40	178
Matthew 10:34-36	110	Matthew 28:18-20	106
Matthew 10:37-39	109	1 Peter 1:8-9	82
Matthew 11:2-6	7	1 Peter 2:24-25	88
Matthew 11:28-30	115	1 Peter 5:5-6	100
Matthew 13:22-23	118	1 Peter 5:8-9	100
Matthew 13:41-43	121	Philippians 2:1-4	151
Matthew 13:47-49	124	Philippians 2:5-8	70
Matthew 14:18-21	127	Philippians 4:6-8	157
Matthew 14:22-25	130	Psalm 1:1-3	163
Matthew 14:29-31	130	Psalm 8:3-4	106
Matthew 15:22-24	133	Psalm 8:5-8	107
Matthew 15:25-28	133	Psalm 22:1-2	76
Matthew 16:15-18	136	Psalm 23:1	88
Matthew 16:21-23	139	Psalm 23:1-4	157
Matthew 16:24-25	139	Psalm 24:3-4	34
Matthew 17:1-4	46	Psalm 40:7-8	28

INDEX OF BIBLE EXTRACTS

Psalm 51:5–6	49	Romans 7:18–20	115
Psalm 67:1–2	133	Romans 8:5–6	118
Psalm 98:7–9	13	Romans 8:14–15	121
Psalm 103:8–14	145	Romans 8:16–17	121
Psalm 118:22	70	Romans 8:38–39	124
Psalm 144:3–4	178	Romans 11:33–36	180
Psalm 145:8–9	115	Romans 12:6–7	136
Psalm 145:14–16	127	Romans 12:8	136
Psalm 145:17–20	127	Romans 12:16–18	139
Psalm 147:16–18	19	Romans 13:9–10	142
Psalm 148:7–10	16	Romans 13:11–12	1
Romans 1:2–4	10	Romans 13:11–14	142
Romans 4:4–5	55	Romans 15:4	5
Romans 5:8–9	58	1 Samuel 16:7	64
Romans 6:12–14	112	1 Thessalonians 2:4–7	163
Romans 6:20–23	112		

Index of Themes

Anticipation, and expectation, 1
Believing the unbelievable, 10
Be prepared, 172
Beyond doubt, 82
Birth and death, 22
Burdens of guilt, 115
Clouds of not knowing, 46
Conundrums of calling, 28
Creation and anxiety, 43
Crumbs of learning, 133
Ends and beginnings, 169
Enough food, 127
Excited understanding, 85
Forgiving ourselves, 145
Fruitful seeds, 118
Grace, truth and rejection, 19
Groping in the dark, 94
Harsh words, 139
Herd instincts, 88
Hidden talents, 175
Humble knowledge, 100
Losing and finding, 109
Loss and discovery, 79
Love and orgies, 142
Meat and drink, 58
Mixed messages, 121
New world order, 4
Painful images, 124
Paths to truth, 91
Patience, 7

Paying our dues, 160
Personal failures, 166
Personal worth, 148
Proper fruit, 154
Prophets of good, 112
Questioning acceptance, 61
Real authority, 151
Reluctant guests, 157
Rhetoric and reason, 31
Rising to new heights, 97
Ritual reminders, 49
Sales talk, 163
Salt and spirit, 37
Seeing and believing, 64
Significant acts, 73
Skills and belief, 136
Sorrowful doubts, 67
Start of life's work, 25
Storms of faith, 130
Struggling thoughts, 34
Tempting offers, 52
Testing times, 16
Touching God, 178
Tough talking, 40
Trappings, traditions and words, 13
Triumph and tragedy, 70
Truth and betrayal, 76
Uncomfortable words, 55
Varieties of gifts, 103
What about God? 106

www.ingramcontent.com/pod-product-compliance
Lightning Source LLC
Chambersburg PA
CBHW071230170426
43191CB00032B/1224